Education
for Work

Education
for Work

*The Historical Evolution
of Vocational and Distributive
Education in America*

Arthur F. McClure
James Riley Chrisman
Perry Mock

Rutherford • Madison • Teaneck
Fairleigh Dickinson University Press
London and Toronto: Associated University Presses

Associated University Presses
440 Forsgate Drive
Cranbury, NJ 08512

Associated University Presses
25 Sicilian Avenue
London WC1A 2QH, England

Associated University Presses
2133 Royal Windsor Drive
Unit 1
Mississauga, Ontario
Canada L5J 1K5

Library of Congress Cataloging in Publication Data

McClure, Arthur F.
   Education for work.

   Bibliography: p.
   Includes index.
   1. Vocational education—United States—History.
2. Distributive education—United States—History.
3. Vocational education—Law and legislation—United
States—History.   I. Chrisman, James Riley, 1941–   .
II. Mock, Perry, 1926–   .   III. Title.
LC1045.M253   1985   370.11′3′0973   83-49203
ISBN   0-8386-3205-X

Printed in the United State of America

To Judy, Barbara, and Lucille—
  Wives, partners, and inspirations

Contents

Preface

This study provides an overview of the history of distributive education and a starting point for students, faculty, and general readers who for professional, academic, or personal reasons are beginning their studies in distributive education. Programs in distributive education have become an accepted part of high schools, community colleges, and four-year colleges throughout the nation. This volume is thus, a combined history, bibliography, and survey guide designed to encourage and further the reader's understanding of distributive education in American life.

In writing this introductory history of distributive education in the United States, we have worked with certain assumptions about the nature of that history, the role of pedagogy, and the students to whom this book is directed. First, we have assumed that there is a need to present an overview of the historical processes which concern the evolution of distributive education as a distinct field. Second, we have assumed that *Education for Work* serves as an introduction to the history of distributive education. Third, we hope that students will be stimulated to pursue specific areas of interest, and, wherever possible, to open further areas for discussion.

Each historical form of distributive education is presented in perspective in order to show how present forms of it have developed out of forms of the past. This book summarizes in non-technical language and without jargon the major trends in the development of distributive education as an important part of vocational education in the United States. Professional educators and scholars know a great deal about the history of distributive education, but a large proportion of what they know is phrased in their technical code and buried in their professional journals. This book then is not written especially for a narrow group of scholars and teachers, but for other educated people who would like to have a broad overview of what we have discovered in our research.

9

It was our aim to present vocational and distributive education in holistic terms by maintaining a balance of its technical, general, positive, and negative aspects. To what extent we have been successful in this endeavor is for the reader to judge.

Many debts were incurred in the writing of this volume. Although we cannot acknowledge personally all those who assisted us, we would like to thank our former student, Roy Kenagy, whose research efforts contributed to our developing knowledge of the history of distributive education. We are also greatly obligated to Mary Helen McCoy, Bonnie Schroder, Ruth Hirner, Dana Piper, and Kay Kerney for their skill and patience in typing the manuscript. We also express our particular indebtedness to our wives who encouraged us when we were discouraged, caught us when we stumbled, pushed us when we lagged, and rejoiced with us when this book was completed. Theirs was the more difficult task.

Arthur F. McClure
James Riley Chrisman
Perry Mock

Education
for Work

1   Vocational Education before Smith-Hughes

Developments in Technical Education

European Background

Education for work among primitive men was accomplished largely through pickup methods of observation and direct imitation, from father to son or from the elders of the society to its youths. Apprenticeship, probably the first organized form of vocational education, reflects this background. The student *apprentice* was bound by a contract to a *master*, who had the obligation to teach him the vocation. The Babylonian Code of Hammurabi, now more than four thousand years old, concisely defines the relationship: "If an artisan take a son for adoption and teach him his handicraft one may not bring claim against him. If he does not teach him his handicraft that son may return to his father's house."[1] Apprenticeship was also practiced to some degree by the Egyptians, Hebrews, Greeks, and Romans, although informal education within the family was probably more important in providing workers for ancient society.[2]

During the late Middle Ages apprenticeship became the basic method of vocational education, through the growth of merchant and craft guilds. Members of each guild held a virtual monopoly over the practice and teaching of their particular trade or profession. To become a member of a guild required a period of apprenticeship under a master in that guild, which usually lasted seven years. There was no other way to legally learn or enter a trade. In addition to providing the apprentice with both vocational and moral instruction, the master also provided food and lodging for his apprentices, generally in the master's own home, where the shops themselves were commonly located. In return, the master received the services of the apprentice for the period specified. If the apprentice progressed satisfactorily he became a journeyman, and then, upon completion of an acceptable *master-piece*, he became a master. The guilds regulated the system, and provided inspectors to search for contract violations. The guilds also provided Latin schools for boys who wanted to continue on into the universities, and apprenticeship schools to supplement the teaching of individual masters. The apprenticeship system gave the guilds an efficient method of maintaining their elite status and at the same time enabled the guilds to cultivate and encourage the craftsmanship characteristic of the Middle Ages.[3]

Merchant guilds were probably the first to be formed, the first appearing in England soon after the Norman conquest. These guilds regulated and presumably provided instruction for all the practices involved in the buying and selling of goods, which included pricing and methods of sale. Historians believe that craftsmen were originally members of the particular merchant guild whose goods they produced and as the industrial processes became more complex and the quality and quantity of goods increased, craft guilds were formed and eventually became more powerful than the merchant guilds. Actually there was little separation between merchant and craftsman. Business practices emphasized the production and transportation of goods, and in the limited market there was no need for the practice of salesmanship in the modern sense of the term. The apprenticeship system thus served primarily as a means of industrial rather than business education—production methods rather than trade was the major problem of the merchant throughout the Middle Ages.[4]

As this problem was solved, the guilds and consequently the apprenticeship system declined in power. In England the Statute of Artificers (1562) codified on the national level the existing local apprenticeship laws. The Poor Law (1601) attempted to relieve the growing unemployment and unrest in the lower classes by providing that the children of the poor could be apprenticed to masters by church wardens and overseers. Even with such official support, by the middle of the 1700s the guilds in England had lost control of the trades; in 1835 the Municipal Reform Bill, which allowed any citizen the right to keep a shop, ended support of the system by the government. This decline was the result of the growth of commerce and the Industrial Revolution, which expanded the demand for goods and at the same time simplified through mechanization the skills required for production. The required seven years of training for an apprentice became meaningless because of the increasing rate of change in production methods, and merchants resorted to importing foreign workers or violating the length of service in order to efficiently obtain skilled workers. Under these circumstances, it was only a matter of time before new methods of education replaced apprenticeship.[5]

Colonial America

At a time when apprenticship was beginning to lose force in England, it became the single most important method of education in the American colonies. No systems of education were established by the colonial governments; instead, individuals were required to provide for the training of those who were dependent on them. Apprenticeship, either voluntary or compulsory, became the principal means of such education. Voluntary apprentices chose their won master and trade; compulsory apprentices were usually the children of the poor, bound out as a means of relief. Because there were no guilds, a contract known as an *indenture* was entered into between apprentice and master. The master, in addition to teaching a trade, was usually required to teach his apprentices reading, writing, and arithmetic. For those masters who could not satisfy this requirement, separate schools were established to which apprentices could be sent. Girls were commonly indentured, but instead of a trade or craft they were taught the duties of housekeeping. Even the professions of lawyer, physician, and schoolmaster were taught through apprenticeship. For all those citizens who did not have the means to send their children to the private schools established by the church, apprenticeship was the only method that could provide an elementary education for their children.[6]

As it had in Europe, the advent of the Industrial Revolution doomed the apprenticeship system in America. During the first third of the nineteenth century, the apprenticeship rapidly lost its value in the United States both as a training and as an educational system. The small shop of a master and his few apprentices changed into a small factory operation. And when the first power loom began operation in 1814, the modern factory era was at hand. By the time the Industrial Revolution burst into full bloom in the United States in the 1860s, the apprenticeship system had been discarded and forgotten. The new technology with its ever-changing knowledge exceeded the ability of the apprentice system to supply enough trained production workers. It was no longer necessary for a single worker to produce a finished product from raw material. The required skills were aimed toward the machines and the adaptation of new procedures to machine use. As the machines and the procedures changed, old skills became obsolete and new ones were developed. In this climate of rapid change, new training processes were also needed.[7]

Early Schools

Publicly the first attempts to establish vocational and industrial education in America were made in New Mexico at the Franciscan Mission Schools. Around 1630, the Franciscans began to offer instruction that combined work and formal education. The students, who were primarily Indians, concentrated their efforts until the age of nine upon mastering the skills of reading, writing, arithmetic, and the fine arts. Once a basic mastery of these subjects had been attained, the emphasis became entirely vocational. Students in the upper age bracket, nine and above, were trained by the Franciscans in classes in carpentry, metalworking, masonry, tailoring, and other skills. Later, the most talented of the students became the teachers of these skills to others. There may have been as many as twenty-five of these Franciscan schools in New Mexico. Tragically, the schools and all their records were destroyed during a rebellion in 1680. However, the Franciscans later established similar schools in Texas, California, and Florida.[8]

While the Franciscan schools were being established in the Southwest, practical courses were introduced into the curriculum in Anglo-America. In 1635, a teacher hired by the Plymouth Colony was instructed to include a class on the casting of accounts. This later became the pattern in a number of schools throughout the New England and Middle Atlantic colonies. Nevertheless in the seventeenth and eighteenth centuries, those who wanted to prepare for a business career continued to find that the best training was through an apprenticeship. More importantly, the concept that practical and formal education could exist in the same curriculum was thoroughly established. The argument from then until the present day was to be the question of what constituted the proper mixture of practical and formal courses.[9]

Franklin's Academy

Tradition, which can act as either a bulwark or an impediment of civilization, became the stumbling block in the development of industrial education in America. One of those whose plans ran afoul of tradition was Benjamin Franklin. In 1749, Franklin published a pamphlet entitled *Proposals Relating to the Education of Youth in Pennsylvania*. He urged the establishment of an academy that would realistically prepare the youth to deal with the problems of making a living. The academy would offer courses under three major divisions—English, Mathematics, and History. Included in the curriculum would be courses designed to prepare the students for a life in commerce. Among these courses would be accounting, history of commerce, and modern languages for merchants. Before the academy was organized, Franklin issued a second pamphlet entitled *Idea of an English School*, in which he proposed a six-year curriculum for boys beginning at the age of eight. Those who entered this English School had to have a basic mastery of reading and writing. The courses that Franklin listed for each of the six years were designed to provide a practical education for a life in commerce. Franklin's plan met with opposition from those who followed what was then the prevailing thought that an education without the study of Latin and the classics did not constitute an education at all. As a result, the academy was organized in 1751 with a Latin School as a more than equal partner of the English School. The ultimate fate of the English School was set from the beginning. The Latin master was the head of the Academy and was paid twice the salary of the English master. Within a few years, the Latin School became dominant and the Academy became a prep school for those wishing to enter college. As the position of the Latin School rose, the English school was gradually reduced to an elementary school and assigned the task of teaching basic reading and writing to little children.[10]

Mechanic's Institute

By the early years of the nineteenth century, the emphasis in industrial education had changed. It has no longer focused on the training of youth to enter into commerce or the trades, but on the improvement of the skills of those who were currently emloyed. This continuation of training took place in evening classes held in what were known as "Mechanic's Institutes." These institutes first appeared in England shortly before 1800. In the 1820s, Mechanic's Institutes were established in the United States. The first was started in New York City by the General Society of Mechanics and Tradesmen (1820). Probably the best known of these institutes was established in Philadelphia (1824) and named honor of Benjamin Franklin—the Franklin Institute. These insti-

tutes and the others that were established followed a similar plan
of instruction, which included a series of evening classes for
adults in such subjects as the physical sciences, mathematics, and
languages. Special classes in various subjects were also organized
upon request. Whereas the instructors were required to lecture in
a manner that would allow those of little education to understand
the classes, a major problem was that even with this effort to
simplify the courses, the material remained beyond the compre-
hension of many students. Improper funding, poor facilities, inadequate teaching materials, few competent teachers, inadequate
teaching methods, and a poor system of selecting students for
particular classes also became insurmountable problems for the
institutes. Whereas Mechanic's Institutes were established in
many American cities, they were never as popular or as successful
in the United States as they were in England.[11]

Lyceums

Although the intent of the Mechanic's Institutes was primarily
to educate urban workers, the Lyceum movement was designed
to aid the tradesmen in small towns and those in agriculture. The
foundation of the American Lyceum is usually credited to Josiah
Holbrook, who in 1826 published a plan for the popular education
of adults. Under this plan, the people of a small town or of an
agricultural area would organize a local lyceum. The local lyceum
would be associated with the state lyceum, which, in turn, would
be a part of the national lyceum. The national lyceum held an
annual convention from 1831 to 1839. By 1833, there were
approximately one thousand lyceums in the United States.[12]

The purpose of the lyceum was to provide an atmosphere and a
meetingplace where workingmen could gather and discuss subjects of interest. Among these were subjects selected from the
sciences, such as mechanics, chemistry, botany, mathematics,
and hydraulics, and subjects from the cultural realm, such as history, politics, and economics. The life of the lyceum movement
was short, and, it succumbed to many of the same maladies that
had earlier beset the Mechanic's Institutes. When the national
lyceum held its last convention in 1839, the movement was
already in decline. Although the movement continued to function
until midcentury, its number and its influence dropped rapidly.
However, part of the lyceum's popular education continued later
in the century through popular lectures and the "Chautauqua
Movement."[13]

Technical Institutes

The desire to improve the skills of the workingman through technical and scientific knowledge fostered the development of technical institutes. This was particularly true of the Rensselaer School—later known as Rensselaer Polytechnic Institute. It was the intention of its founder, Stephen Van Rensselaer, to establish a school in the sciences and trained to apply their scientific knowledge to the everyday problems that confronted the farmer and the workingman. Once so trained, the teachers were to conduct lectures and evening classes in rural areas and in small towns for the farmers and the tradesmen. From the time of its establishment in 1824, few of Rensselaer's graduates ever ventured into the country to conduct such classes. The curriculum, as envisioned by Rensselaer, emphasized science and its practical application. Rensselaer also recognized a need for realistic laboratory experience. With this in mind, he arranged for the students to work, observe, and to try new techniques at some of the better farms and workshops in the area. Thus the students at Rensselaer School received what was then the best of two worlds—quality scientific training and the opportunity to give it a practical application.[14] Other schools were started with the intent to emphasize the practical application of science, but few were as successful as Rensselaer's. Those technical institutes that were successful were not organized until after the Civil War—e.g. Worcester, Massachusetts, Polytechnic Institute (1868); Case School of Applied Science, Cleveland, Ohio (1881); and the California School of Mechanical Arts, San Francisco (1895).[15]

As the Industrial Revolution gathered speed, there was a growing desire among some American educators and industrialists to change the basic curriculum offered in the schools. Although their goals were not the same, each usually found an ally in the other. The educators were interested in expanding the scope of education, whereas the businessmen were concerned with how education could provide them with better-trained employees. The result was if businessmen wanted the addition of a subject to the educational program, they usually found a number of educators who were willing to listen and do it. This was the case concerning the addition of drawing to the curriculum; when businessmen wanted it, they found eager allies among some of the educators.[16]

German Drawing Schools

   Probably the most important impetus for the addition of drawing came from the influence of the German drawing schools and
the success of German industries. The Centennial Exposition
held at Philadelphia in 1876 featured displays of machinery and
finished goods from numerous countries. One exhibit that was
viewed with admiration by American businessmen was one that
depicted German industry. This display emphasized machinery
and the practical use of science, part of which was shown through
the use of drawings, charts, and diagrams depicting machines and
mechanical processes. As a result, American businessmen began
to call for the inclusion of drawing into the curriculum of American schools. Art education for practical use had been a part of
German education as early as 1780, when a school was established
as part of the art academy at Augsburg with the goal of using
design to improve the production of goods. Drawing had been a
part of the program in some of the American schools, but businessmen called for a change in its emphasis. The businessmen
wanted the drawing program to stress the practical rather than
the artistic and they were interested in drawing as a means of improving the students' grasp of machines and mechanical principles.
The businessmen wanted drawing taught in a manner that would
encourage the development of draftsmen and engineers. This,
they felt, would be good for business. As a result of such pressure
from businessmen, drawing was added to the programs of most
schools including the public high schools, and evening classes
were offered in drawing. By the turn of the twentieth century, the
interest and emphasis on drawing—particularly in the evening
classes—had all but vanished. However, drawing had made its
contribution to the concept of practical education for vocational
training.[17]

Russian Manual Training

   The Philadelphia Exposition of 1876 was also responsible for
another change in American technical education, the adoption of
the Russian system of shop training. The Russian exhibit at Philadelphia contained a display from the Moscow Imperial Technical School, in which the organization and use of a training shop for
technical school students was outlined. Prior to 1868, the Moscow
Imperial Technical School had operated in basically the same
manner as most other technical schools, including those in the

United States. Laboratory experience, if any, for the students was obtained through school shops that were designed to produce a product for the retail market. Such shops tended to be expensive, produced low-quality goods, and lost money because the students received their basic training in the use and care of the tools while they were engaged in the production of the goods. Therefore, quality suffered, sales were low, and expenses soared. In 1868, the director of the Moscow Imperial Technical School— Victor Della Vos—conceived the idea of a separate training shop in which beginning students would be taught the basics, e.g., the care of tools and machines, basic production operations, and the application of the tools to the production operations. Della Vos constructed training shops for several skills, which were so successful and less expensive that the Moscow Imperial Technical School soon dropped all of its production shops.[18]

One of those influenced by the Russian display was the president of Massachusetts Institute of Technology, John D. Runkle, who shortly after examining the Russian exhibit, recommended the system to the trustees of his institution. In August 1876, the trustees gave their approval and Runkle immediately ordered the establishment of training shops not only for the engineering classes but also for the manual and industrial courses. The Russian training shops, including those established in American schools, were very formal. The shop was so structured with its lectures, teacher-selected exercises, demonstrations, instruction sheets, and illustrations that there was little or no room left for student creativity. Nevertheless, it did perform its goal—the orderly transmission to the student of basic knowledge and skills.[19]

Sloyd System

The Russian system, although better than previous training methods, contained some serious flaws. With its emphasis on specific exercises, it was so highly structured and formal that only the older or most dedicated students managed to maintain their interest. Often the projects which the students completed offered little in the way of beauty or function. In an effort to maintain student interest, European and American schools turned to a Scandinavian system known as the Sloyd system. This system, which was based on the Scandinavian tradition of home handicraft, was deemed to be better than the Russian training procedures for the younger students—particularly those in elementary schools. The Sloyd system emphasized the physical and mental development of the child as well as the acquisition of skills. It also approached the task in terms of the student's completing an entire project that combined beauty and usefulness, and relied on highly trained teachers rather than artisans as the instructors. The Sloyd system was first introduced in the United States in 1884 and it soon became very popular in American schools. By 1894, the United States Commissioner of Education reported that twenty-five precent of all the schools offering manual arts in grades seven through twelve used the Sloyd system. However, critics soon charged the Sloyd method with some of the same flaws as the Russian system. Primarily these were charges that the Sloyd system was inflexible and too highly structured.[20]

Arts and Crafts

One attempt to correct the inflexibility of the Russian and Sloyd systems was through the Arts and Crafts Movement, which started in England in the last part of the nineteenth century as a protest to the poor workmanship of previous training methods. The movement was introduced into American schools about the same time as the Russian and Sloyd systems, and it placed greater emphasis on creativity and beauty rather than on the acquisition of skills. As criticism of the Russian and Sloyd systems grew, many of the ideas of the Arts and Crafts Movement were integrated into the manual arts programs. It emphasized the use of many types of materials other than wood, such as leather and metal. Furthermore, it encouraged the student to be creative through such things as modeling, carving, and drawing. As a result, many of the old formal skill exercises were dropped from the programs of younger students. The Arts and Crafts Movement brought an increased measure of flexibility to the American versions of the Russian and Sloyd systems.[21]

Pestalozzi and Von Fellenberg

The influence of Europe was also felt in American education through the philosophies of two Swiss educators—Johann Heinrich Pestalozzi (1746–1827) and Philip Emanuel Von Fellenberg (1771–1844). Their influence on vocational and general education was important from the eighteenth century to the present. Pestalozzi, who has been called the "father of manual training" and is considered the founder of modern educational methodology, established a series of schools in which manual work was combined with general education. Pestalozzi believed the way to alleviate poverty was to train the children of the poor in work skills. At the same time it was equally important to cultivate their minds and social consciences. In fact, he believed that an education that emphasized only one side—either vocational or general—created an individual who was of little value to society. Such a person was either fit only for the earning of his living or was out of step with his environment. Pestalozzi's first school, Neuhof, was a farm where he took poor children into his family, cared for them, trained them in handicrafts and farming, and gave them a general education. This school, like most of the others he established, was an educational triumph but a financial disaster. As Pestalozzi developed his methodology, drawing became an integral part of the curriculum. He used drawing as a means to sharpen the students' powers of observation and description, but its importance as a factor in industrial education later increased the appeal of Pestalozzian pedagogy.[22]

Von Fellenberg, while using some of the educational methods of Pestalozzi, differed with him in several ways. Von Fellenberg believed that the levels of society represented a natural separation of people according to their ability. Consequently, individuals could best be educated and trained within their own groups. However, each group should also be taught to understand and respect the position and function of the other groups. Therefore, Von Fellenberg's school was organized along social lines. The school had an academy for the sons of the elite, a school of applied science for the sons of the middle classes, and a farm and trade school for the sons of the poor. Von Fellenberg's greatest contribution probably came in the field of school administration and organization. He selected skills that were necessary to the efficient operation of the school and its farm. He hired skilled people to perform these jobs and to teach the students. As a result, his school was a financial as well as an educational success. Von Fellenberg's school proved that the proper organization and management of work could pay the bills and train students for vocations. His success influenced the establishment of other work-oriented programs in orphanages and reform schools.[23]

Calvin M. Woodward and the Manual Training School of
Washington University

American vocational education in the latter part of the
nineteenth century was shaped by the impact of the Russian system, the Sloyd system, the Arts and Crafts Movement, and the
European pedagogical philosophies. Certain American educators
quickly accepted these ideas and adapted them to the American
situation. One of these men was Calvin Milton Woodward, dean
of the Polytechnic faculty, Washington University, St. Louis.
From about 1870, Woodward had his engineering students at
Washington University use a shop and tools to construct models
that illustrated certain mechanical principles. Throughout the
1870s, he continually expanded the scope of this program. When
Woodward was introduced to the Russian system of training in
1876, he quickly grasped its value to the engineering students. He
also thought that the extension of a shop system into the secondary schools would provide skill training to students during an
important period of their lives. Woodward believed that the inclusion of shop training courses in the high school would provide
a much needed instruction in the use of basic tools. Such skills
would give the student a degree of flexibility when they chose a
vocation. These basic skills were common to a variety of jobs. It
was Woodward's contention that the school shops which taught
particular trades locked the student into a vocational choice
that might be overcrowded by the time he had finished school.
Woodward also believed that such job-oriented training created
a worker who knew only those things connected with his particular vocational selection. The proper vocational education would
concentrate on the basics, familiarize the student with the scientific principles involved, and also provide him with a general
education.[24]

In September 1880, Washington University opened the Manual
Training School for boys fourteen years and older. The school
provided a complete educational program with instruction in
science, mathematics, language, literature, history, drawing, and
shopwork. A certain amount of prestige was connected with gaining admission to the school. It developed a reputation as a tough
school that accepted only the best effort from its students. Candi-
dates for admission to the school were tested for their knowledge
of mathematics, geography, grammar, spelling, and penmanship.
As a result, the student body may not have accurately represented a true cross section of the age group it was intended to

serve. Woodward, however, believed that the concept of combining general education with vocational training would make for an educational process that was more interesting and would thus encourage more students to enter and complete a secondary education. In particular, he believed that the dropout rate of the high schools would decline as this type of vocational education became more available. The Manual Training School of Washington University functioned well for thirty-three years. In 1915, declining enrollment forced the university to close the school. The school's demise can be credited to its success. By 1915, the public high schools of St. Louis had accepted the concept of the Vocational School and had developed similar programs of their own. By the time the Manual Training School closed, Woodward's basic concept of vocational education in the secondary schools was an accepted part of American education.[25]

Cooperative Training

Herman S. Schneider, a civil engineer and a member of the Lehigh University faculty, believed that the education of engineers lacked an essential ingredient—practical experience. By 1901, Schneider developed a plan that called for the student to split his time between formal classes and actual job experience. Schneider believed that the experience obtained by working in an engineering capacity for a company would provide the student with practical experience. Opposition by his colleagues at Lehigh was so stubborn that Schneider realized the plan would not be workable there. He accepted a position with the University of Cincinnati, and he was later able to get the School of Engineering at Cincinnati to let him try his plan on a limited scale. The plan first used during the 1906–1907 school year by a small number of engineering students. Under the cooperative plan, the students worked in pairs with one working while the other remained in class. The two students switched every week between work and study. The plan was a success and by 1927 the number of universities and colleges using cooperative training as a part of their engineering programs had grown to between twenty and twenty-five.[26]

Schneider's cooperative plan was probably first introduced into the high school curriculum in 1908 at Fitchburg, Massachusetts. In the spring of that year, Schneider spoke about his plan to a meeting of manufacturers, one of whom, Daniel Simonds, became so excited by the concept that upon his return home to

Fitchburg he began contacting other manufacturers about it. As a result of their interest and pressure, an industrial cooperative training program was started in the high school at Fitchburg in September 1908. Cooperative training was on its way to becoming an accepted part of American vocational education. It was to become a major feature in the development of modern commercial vocation education. Distributive education in the modern secondary schools is based in part on Schneider's concept of cooperative training.[27]

Vocational Education of Minorities

Another important development during the late nineteenth century was the increased interest in vocational training for minorities, primarily black Americans and American Indians. Immediately following the end of the Civil War, the nation was faced with the problem of how to accommodate the ex-slaves. Most of those in positions of power believed the new freedman possessed few of the skills necessary for full involvement in American life. Owing to the nature of their previous condition, the vast majority of the former slaves entered freedom unskilled, uneducated, and unprepared. One of the first to wrestle with this problem was an administrator with the Freedman's Bureau, General Samuel Chapman Armstrong. General Armstrong was not a typical Union officer in that he had considerable experience in dealing with blacks and their problems. One of his assignments in the Civil War had been as commander of the Eighth Regiment of United States Colored Troops. In the spring of 1868, Armstrong opened a boarding school for young freedmen at Hampton, Virginia. Armstrong envisioned an institution that would provide a practical education, a blend of the general and the vocational. It was his desire that those trained in Hampton Institute would go back to their homes and train their fellow blacks. In this manner, and over an extended period of time, the level of skills and the quality of life among black Americans would be raised to the point that they could enter the mainstream of American life.[28]

In 1872, a young freedman from the mines of West Virginia entered Hampton Institute: Booker T. Washington enrolled in the institute with a minimum of education; he graduated filled with the conviction that Armstrong's philosophy pointed the way for black Americans. Washington accepted Armstrong's philosophy, expanded on it, and became its most articulate advocate. Tuskegee Insitute, which Washington founded in 1881 as a normal school, perpetuated this vocational philosophy. The students at Tuskegee were required to work and develop skills as well as attend classes.[29]

In 1895, the Cotton States and International Exposition was held in Atlanta. Washington was asked to give a five-minute address before one of the sessions. This speech, later called the "Atlanta Compromise," had a tremendous impact upon race relations and minority vocational education. In his speech, Washington proposed a cessation of any quest for social equality between the races. He called upon black Americans to concentrate their efforts upon developing skills, building character through work, and raising the level of their education. In essence, Washington told the southern whites that he would accept segregation if they would support his and Armstrong's vocational philosophy. The "Atlanta Compromise" was loudly acclaimed by southern leaders, both white and black. One result of Washington's plan was that some state governments lost some of their reluctance to appropriate money for black educational institutions. Political leaders in the South who had actively opposed spending money to educate blacks found that once the threat of social equality between the races was removed they could support the establishment and the financial backing of vocational schools for blacks.[30]

Vocational education became the motivating force in many respects behind the establishment of schools for minorities in the last decades of the nineteenth century. The concept of work, study, and training was also used in the schools established for Indians—Carlisle school in 1878 and Haskell Institute in 1884, In these schools, as in Hampton Institute, the goal was to train students who would go back to their people and teach them the skills they had learned. The success of these vocational school for blacks and Indians also advanced the development of vocational education for white students. By the end of the century, the white community was enough aware of these successful schools to demand that their children be given similar opportunities for vocational training.[31]

Public High Schools

Vocational training was not the only part of the American educational system to undergo change in the late nineteenth century. One of the other important changes came in the public high school. Prior to the development of the manual training schools in the 1880s, the American high school was a preparatory school for those who planned to enter college. That this was its primary function is illustrated by the fact that in 1870 sixty percent of all high school graduates eventually earned a college degree. A high school education was not considered as terminal, and it was not considered as a means of preparation for the student to face life and its problems. But after 1880, a profound change occurred in the way the American populace viewed the high school and its duties. Attendance in the high school jumped spectacularly after 1880, partly as a result of the enactment by a number of states of child labor laws and compulsory school attendance laws. By 1890, such laws had been enacted by about half of the states, and all of the states had them by 1920. As a result, both attendance and graduation from high schools doubled in every decade from 1880 through the first third of the twentieth century. However, whereas the number of students grew after 1870, the percentage of the nation's fourteen to seventeen year olds in high school by 1890 was only seven percent. As the number of those who attended and graduated from high school increased, the number of high school graduates who later earned a college degree decreased. This figure dropped from sixty per cent in 1870 to under twenty per cent for the decade of 1910–1920. The high school diploma had become the terminal degree in American education.[32]

As the number of the students who attended and graduated from high school increased, the colleges were able to raise their entrance requirements. Concurrent with this, the vocational and manual training programs in the colleges became more and more a part of the training for professionals such as engineers, scientists, and agriculturalists. This in turn accentuated the need for people who were trained in skills in the middle-level range. One reaction to this increased demand was the inclusion of vocational training in the high school curriculum. Because of the increased enrollments, the high school seemed a natural place to teach vocational skills. The first high school of this type was the Manual Training School of Washington University. Others followed and the first manual training high school founded as a part of the public school system was opened in Baltimore in 1884. As the nineteenth century drew to a close, the number of publicly supported manual high schools and the number of high schools that included manual training in their general curriculum grew. By 1900, the public school system in over one hundred cities included manual training in the curriculum of their high schools. However, the complete acceptance of vocational training as a part of the general high school curriculum did not come until the twentieth century.[33]

Philosophy of Vocational Education at the Turn of the Century

By the beginning of the twentieth century, most American educational theorists and school administrators agreed upon the value of vocational education. The problem centered around their often heated disagreement as to *where* and *how* vocational skills should be taught. Vocationalists such as Calvin Woodward believed that vocational education should be an integral part of the curriculum of the high schools. Others of a more traditional inclination, such as William T. Harris, the United States Commissioner of Education from 1889 to 1906, argued that vocational training did not belong in high school curriculum. They believed that the time needed to teach skills could only be obtained by shortening the amount of time spent on the traditional subjects— languages, history, mathematics, and others. To these advocates, the inclusion of vocational education into the curriculum of any high school weakened the school's effort to achieve the primary goal of providing a cultural education. These opponents, who included Harris, proposed that vocational education be offered through separate vocational high schools.[34]

The controversy that ensued over the place of vocational education in the high school curriculum was so thorny a problem that leading educational theorists devoted much time and thought to the matter. Foremost among these philosophers was the famous John Dewey of the University of Chicago. Through his observations and experimentations, Dewey provided the telling philosophical and psychological justification for the learning-by-doing approach to education of Armstrong, Woodward, and Washington. Dewey was very concerned about the place of vocational education in the curriculum, and he stated repeatedly that vocational education belonged in the general curriculum of the schools. His greatest fear was that a dualism would develop in American education with one school for those who followed traditional goals and one for those interested in obtaining a vocational education. In such a dualism, Dewey thought that society would consider one school to be superior and the other inferior. Thus, one group of students would develop an inflated sense of self-value while they considered the other group as their social inferiors. Of greater concern to Dewey was his belief that dualism would lead to such a high degree of specialization that neither

school would provide a well-rounded education. As Dewey saw
it, the only way to avoid this was through a comprehensive curriculum that provided both types of education in the same school.
Dewey's warnings were not heeded. With the exception of a
few business education courses, home economics, general shop
classes, and—in rural schools—agriculture, most vocational
education was assigned to separate schools.[35]

Development of Retail Salesmanship Programs

Background in Business and Commercial Education

As previously noted, business classes were the first vocational
education courses introduced into the curriculum of American
schools. Starting with the instructions of the Plymouth Colony in
1635, which was concerned with the teaching of casting accounts,
the teaching of business subjects over the years gradually spread
throughout the country. By the early 1700s, bookkeeping was a
part of the curriculum of schools in New York and Pennsylvania.
One goal of Franklin's academy was to train its students in business and commercial subjects, and the teaching of bookkeeping
was required in the high schools of Massachusetts by law after
1827.[36]

In the last half of the nineteenth century, the most important
sources of business education were the business schools, most of
which were privately operated schools. The United States Bureau
of Education estimated that there were about 373 business
schools with an enrollment in excess of 115,000 by the end of the
century. The quality of instruction in these schools varied greatly
between the schools and teachers. Some of the schools were of
poor quality and existed for only a year or so. However, others
built a reputation for quality instruction and operated successfully
for many years. The typical curriculum for these schools included
penmanship, bookkeeping, commercial law, business arithmetic,
spelling, shorthand, grammar, composition, and economics. In
the first half of the nineteenth century, the business training
obtained through these schools was viewed as a supplement to a
regular employee's on-the-job work experience. In the last half of
the century, the business training obtained in these schools was
viewed as a means of becoming qualified for employment.[37]

Whereas a few business and commercial classes had been a part
of the curriculum of the public school for years, it was not until

after 1890 that the public high schools began to offer vocational programs in business. In most cases, these courses resulted from pressure created by popular demand and not from the desire by educators to improve the curriculum. Enrollment in these courses grew rapidly. By 1893, the enrollment was estimated at over 15,000. Seventeen years later in 1910, approximately 1,440 public high schools were offering vocational courses in business. These high school courses enrolled more than 81,000 students. Even this phenomenal growth rate, however, did not allow the public high schools to supplant the private business schools as the major source of business training. The private schools in 1910 numbered approximately 541 with more than 134,000 students. The enrollment in business courses in the public high schools did not exceed that in the private schools until after 1920. Not only did the enrollment of business students in the public high schools lag during this period, the quality of training was considered inferior to that obtained in the private business schools. Private business schools were the first to adopt new methods and procedures such as shorthand, typewriting, and journal publications. Also, the authorship of business textbooks was dominated by those who taught in the private schools until well into the 1920s. For years the business programs in the public high schools were imitations of those in the private schools, and they were usually poor imitations.[38]

As with the other vocational programs, a movement developed with both proponents and opponents of vocational education working for the same goal. Those who were interested in the promotion of vocational business education and those who were interested in the preservation of the traditional high school curriculum jointly advocated the establishment of separate commercial high schools within the public school systems. The first such high school was the Business High School of Washington, D.C., founded in 1890. Other commercial high schools established at the turn of the century were Central High School of Philadelphia in 1898 and the High School of Commerce in New York in 1901. Separate commercial high schools soon followed in Pittsburgh, Chicago, Brooklyn, and Boston. A general pattern among these schools was the omission of the classical studies and the concentration on the vocational studies. The practical subjects that could be applied to commerce, such as grammar, arithmetic, and composition, were also a vital part of the curriculum of these schools.[39]

The last decade of the nineteenth century also marked the beginnings of retail training. Stores, like other types of business and industrial operations, grew in size as technology and the population increased. As the size of retail operations grew, the close tie between the owner-operator and his employees stretched and finally snapped. It was no longer possible for the proprietor to train, observe, and evaluate each employee. The result was that most retail training became a matter of the new employee's trial-and-error experience. Some stores, however, did institute brief training programs for their new employees, which were designed to acquaint the employees with the basic operations of the store.[40]

Training for those who had been employed by the stores for sometime was even slower in its development. As management found otherwise faithful and trusted employees to be deficient in areas that would improve their work, they cast about for ways to overcome these problems. Sometimes the solution lay in retraining them in a new business technique. For others, the difficulties required remedial training in the basics of education—grammar, arithmetic, and spelling to name a few. Probably the first company to establish such a program for its employees was the Wanamaker Company. In 1896, it organized the John Wanamaker Commercial Institute in its Philadelphia store. This school offered not only business courses but also basic education classes similar to those taught in the elementary and high schools. Other companies soon followed Wanamaker's example. Gradually these schools dropped the general education courses and concentrated on highly specific courses in sales procedures, management techniques, and retail organizations.[41]

Lucinda Prince and Department Store Training

An important development in the history of retail training occurred in the fall of 1905, when Lucinda Wayland Prince organized a training class in retail selling for young women. Mrs. Prince was a member of the executive committee of the Women's Educational and Industrial Union of Boston—an organization interested in the educational, vocational, and social problems of women workers. She had gained considerable experience dealing with the young employed women of Boston through her activities as a social worker. While she worked in this capacity, she had noticed that most of the women in retail sales were generally unhappy and poorly paid. Upon further investigation, she found that they were inadequately trained and, as a result, they had little interest either in their jobs or in doing them properly. In an effort to discover if attitude could affect job performance, Mrs. Prince took a sales position in a department store. She studied her merchandise and made an effort to please the customer. As a result, on her first day she sold three times more than the woman who worked the same counter with her. This experience further convinced Mrs. Prince that training and attitude could improve sales. She concluded that if a woman sold more goods, she would unquestionably be of more value to her employer and therefore worthy of a raise.[42]

Mrs. Prince tried to convince the store owners and managers to let her train their sales personnel. As a group, management officers tended to believe that selling could not be taught and that such training probably would not improve the perfomance of the workers. The union, however, agreed to let Mrs. Prince run a pilot program, but management refused to participate. The first class, which started in the fall of 1905, consisted of eight young women whose young age and lack of training would not allow them to be employed in the stores. Upon completion of the class, they found employment as stock girls. The second class, with six older and more qualified young women, was organized in January 1906. Throught Mrs. Prince's constant efforts, the William Filene's Sons Company agreed to let her bring her students into the store one day a week to acquire some practical work experience. As a result of the performance of this class and the growing interest among the merchants, a number of stores agreed to participate in the program when the third class with seven young women began in July 1906. The stores agreed to refer to the school, now called the School of Salesmanship, any job applicant who showed promise but was not qualified because of inexperience. If the applicant was accepted by the school, the store then allowed the school to place the student in the store on Mondays as a salesperson. The student was paid a nominal wage that allowed her to earn some income and to gain experience at the same time. The store also agreed to hire the student on a probationary basis upon her completion of the training. If her performance during the period of probation was satisfactory, she was hired as a permanent employee.[43]

As she gained experience in conducting these classes, Mrs. Prince realized that the students needed more practical experience. The schedule was rearranged so that the students spent the mornings at the school studying sales technique, merchandising, business arithmetic, and other related subjects, and the afternoons were spent working in the stores. The program was so successful that in the fall of 1907 the stores agreed to pay the students full wages while they were enrolled in the school.[44]

The popularity of Mrs. Prince's training techniques grew among the stores as her students continued to demonstrate its value. The graduates of Mrs. Prince's school gained a reputation for their efficiency. One unnamed graduate was credited with decreasing her store's monthly average of mistakes from 30,000 to 3,000 during the first six months of her employment. Another graduate cut the daily rate of mistakes from 600 to 25 within her first nine months on the job. This represented a savings to the stores because less time and money was spent in finding and correcting such mistakes.[45]

Because of the growing interest in her sales training program, in 1911 Mrs. Prince organized a program to train educational directors for stores and to train high school teachers to teach courses in salesmanship. The following year she was asked to organize a sales-training program for girls in a Boston public high school. As with her School of Salesmanship, the merchants agreed to cooperate with Mrs. Prince and to give the high school students the opportunity to gain work experience. Thus, a form of distributive education arrived on the high school scene. The School of Salesmanship was reorganized as the Prince School for Store Service and later became a graduate division of Simmons College. Mrs. Prince remained as director of the school until her death in 1937.[46]

Frederick G. Nichols and Distributive Education

Frederick G. Nichols, director of business education for the public school system of Rochester, New York, developed an interest in the cooperative training concept of Herman Schneider and the retail sales training of Lucinda Prince. In his position that he held from 1913 to 1918, Nichols was able to create a cooperative clerical training program that followed Schneider's pattern of alternating students every week between classwork and on-the-job training. Later, in 1915, Nichols developed a cooperative sales training program, which followed the concepts initiated by Lucinda Prince.[47]

Although Nichols' contribution as a developer of vocational business programs is important, his most influencial contributions probably came after he left the public school system. In 1918 he was appointed to the newly created Federal Board for Vocational

Education as assistant director for business education. He used the influence of this office to promote all vocational business education. However, he seems to have emphasized cooperative programs and retail sales training: distributive education. He left this post in 1920 and in 1922 accepted an appointment at Harvard University as an associate professor of education. There, until his retirement in 1944, his primary duties involved the training of business teachers. Nichols also actively promoted distributive education in his instruction and his writing. Thus, through his activities as a bureaucrat, a teacher, and a writer, Nichols was an important influence for the promotion of cooperative business training programs in the secondary schools all over the United States.[48]

The Spread of High School Programs

Prior to the passage of the Smith-Hughes Act of 1917, distributive education programs were established in only a few public high schools. Among these were schools in Cincinnati, Providence, Boston, Rochester, Chicago, Los Angeles, New York City, Oakland, New Haven, Galesburg (Illinois), Logansport (Indiana), and Worcester (Massachusetts). Although an argument exists among historians concerning which of these cities initiated the first high school program, nearly all of them were founded during the second decade of the twentieth century. Evidence indicates that teachers from Cincinnati and Providence, who were trained by Mrs. Prince in the spring of 1911, returned to their high school that fall and organized retail training programs with work experience. Whatever the order, Cincinnati, Providence, and Boston were the first cities to place distributive education in their public school curriculum. However, the growth of distributive education was slow. Prejudice from both those in traditional education and those in other types of business education was a major impediment. Also, there was a concern among large numbers of parents that retail sales was not a respectable vocation. These attitudes in addition to regulations that concerned the number of hours of class work, the number of hours of employment, and admission policies kept the enrollment down. By 1934 the nationwide enrollment in distributive education in four-year high schools was only 9,508 of a total of 4,496,514 students—less than one-quarter of 1 percent.[49]

Development of State Vocational Programs

The Massachusetts Example

Massachusetts Commissions. In 1905 and 1906, the first effort was made by a state to determine the vocational education needs of its children, and to define the responsibility of the state concerning vocational education. In that year, the legislature of Massachusetts authorized the establishment of a commission to study the needs of education in the state. The commission was particularly instructed to examine the education and the various skills needed in the various industries within the state. In accordance with the instructions of the legislature, the commission was appointed by Governor William L. Douglas, and as a result, it was popularly known as the Douglas Commission. A series of public hearings as held throughout the state, and the public was invited to participate. The commission found that there was concern among the public for the state of vocational in Massachusetts. When the commission published its findings, it noted that there was a shortage of workmen possessing both skill and industrial intelligence, that an extensive interest prevailed in Massachusetts concerning vocational training, and the consensus seemed to be that the vocational education should be supported financially in part—if not entirely—by the state.[50]

The commission also reported that within the state approximately 25,000 youngsters between the ages of fourteen and sixteen were not in school and were either working or idle. However, most of those in this group who were employed were not engaged in an activity that would teach them a trade, but were generally doing menial tasks. The commission referred to the two years between the ages of fourteen and sixteen for this group as wasted years. These young people were not in school and they were not learning a trade. The evidence indicated that the families of not more than 33 percent of the twenty-five thousand youngsters actually needed them to work. For the remaining two-thirds, the decision to leave school centered on their boredom and dissatisfaction with education. The commission believed that if the curriculum reflected a more practical approach to life through vocational education, then those who might leave school could be enticed to stay until they reached age sixteen. Once the youngsters and their parents were shown the practical advantages of staying in school and acquiring vocational skills, those wasted years would become useful years.[51]

The Douglas commission made two specific recommendations. First, it recommended that instruction in the elementary grades be changed to encourage the development of skills needed in an industrial society. It continued to state that instruction in mathematics and the sciences be organized to show its application to industrial society. Second, the commission recommended that an act be passed by the legislature which would establish a second commission to establish and oversee a statewide system of vocational schools. These schools would be parallel to but separate from the existing public school systems. Thus a dual approach to education would be established in Massachusetts.[52]

The state legislature approved an act based on the recommendations of the commission. In the summer of 1906, Governor Douglas appointed a new commission to carry out the provisions of the act. Although the new commission established a vocational education system in Massachusetts, its effectiveness was hampered after it became embroiled in the old arguments concerning the place and scope of vocational training in Amercian education. The commission worried about and argued over such things as: Was training for employment a matter for the public schools? Should public money be spent on vocational training? Did the public have a responsibility to prepare its children for work? If the answer to any of the previous questions is yes, then to what extent should the commission go to provide these services? As a result, all of this internal arguing and indecisiveness caused the rate of development in vocational education in Massachusetts not to meet expected schedules. Because of this, the legislature in 1909 dissolved the commission and merged its functions into the State Board of Education. Although this action ended the dualism in administration, the dual system of schools continued in Massachusetts. The local vocational schools remained separate from and not controlled by the local public school systems.[53]

The Massachusetts Program. The Massachusetts legislature also charged the commission to establish with local consent such day, part-time, and evening schools as were necessary to further the opportunities for vocational training in the state. During its brief existence, the commission established four day vocational schools and sixteen evening schools. These schools provided training in agriculture, industrial trades, and homemaking. The Massachusetts vocational program slowly developed a concept in vocational agriculture that later became the standard practice throughout the United States. In 1908, a system of school and farm-home cooperation was devised. This allowed the agriculture student who lived on a farm with his parents to develop a farm project that he managed under the supervision of his parents and his instructor. Such a supervised project relieved him of the usual obligation of doing agricultural labor on a school-approved farm. This system is still an important part of vocational agriculture.[54]

The basic mode of operation of the Massachusetts vocational education program also set a precedent that other states tended to follow. In Massachusetts the schools were organized by the local areas with state approval. Once the schools were established, curriculum developed, teachers employed, and classes started, the state would reimburse the local organization in the amount of one-half of the expenses incurred for each program, provided that all phases of each program met the requirements of the state. In the beginning there was some discrimination in the granting of state aid based on the type of school. For example, nearly all of the day-school programs received state aid, mainly in the field of agriculture, industrial training, and homemaking. Industrial training offered through evening schools was eligible for state aid. However, homemaking programs available to working women through evening schools were not so eligible. The thinking seemed to be that working women had surrendered their right to be considered as homemakers, and had exchanged it for their job outside of the home, which had become their primary vocation. Fortunately by 1911, this attitude had changed. People came to realize that many working women had dual roles, and that they could profit from courses in homemaking. In that year, the law was changed to allow state aid to be granted for approved evening courses which enrolled working women.[55]

In 1911, Massachusetts also raised the age of compulsory school attendance. The new law required that all children between the ages of fourteen and sixteen attend school, even if they had daytime employment. Working children in this age group were required to attend a minimum of four hours of class instruction per day. However, an effort was made to allow them to work and to get the minimum amount of education. The local schools were instructed to arrange classes for working children between the hours of 7:00 A.M. and 6:00 P.M.[56]

Development in Other States

Massachusetts was not alone in its early efforts to establish a state system of vocational education. Four other states—New Jersey (1911), New York (1909), Connecticut (1909), and Wisconsin (1911)—led the movement along with Massachusetts (1906). These five states developed concepts and organizations that other states quickly imitated. The programs for vocational education established in these five states contained some general similarities. They established some or all of the usual types of vocational schools—day, evening, and part-time. The vocational education and the types of skills that were taught originated from preliminary commissions which first studied the needs of each state. Each state maintained a certain amount of control over either one or all of the following: school administration, finances, and curriculum.[57]

The Wisconsin Programs

Probably the most unique system established by any of the pioneering states was that created by Wisconsin. The laws that governed vocational education in Wisconsin were considered the most complete of any state west of New York. Wisconsin's laws later served as a pattern for many of the midwestern states. As early as 1907, Wisconsin passed legislation that enabled local school districts to organize trade schools, which would be controlled by a separate board known as the committee on trade schools. This committee was appointed by the local school board, and its five members had to be experienced in at least one of the trades taught in the trade school. With approval of the school board, the committee controlled all expenditures, hired all teachers, established the curriculum, and arranged for the buildings and tools necessary for the courses. The school board was empowered by the law to set a tax levy for support of the trade schools. These schools were to be open for boys aged sixteen and older. However, the age requirement was lowered to age fourteen in 1909.[58]

The Wisconsin legislature revised the laws governing vocational education in 1911. Under this law, a state system was established with a State Board of Industrial Education to act as a coordinating body. All state aid was controlled by the state board, which consisted of six members appointed by the governor. The law required that three of the members of the board had to be employers and the remaining three had to be from the ranks of skilled labor. This requirement helped to calm the fears of both management and labor that one might use the training system to the detriment of the other.[59]

The act of 1911 also required all towns with a population of five thousand or more to create a local Board of Industrial Education.

This board would be appointed by local school officials, and its membership was divided between labor and management, two of the members had to be employers and two had to be skilled laborers. This board was given more autonomy than the previous one established by the law of 1907 as well as local control over all vocational financing. State aid could only be granted upon the board's approval. Local funds could not be spent without its endorsement, and the board also determined the local tax levy. The local board also hired and fired teachers, purchased all supplies, arranged for buildings and tools, and determined the curriculum. However, the curriculum had to be approved by the state superintendent of Education and the State Board of Industrial Education. If state approval was given, the state board then determined the allotment of state aid. This law not only relieved some of the animosity between management and labor concerning vocational education but also made it virtually impossible for those in traditional education to control or weaken the vocational program. Needless to say, the system was not popular among some in traditional education who viewed with alarm the dualism and the splitting of financial control created by the system.[60]

2   The Smith-Hughes Act

Background of Federal Aid to Education

Ordinance of 1787

In many ways national aid to education is as old as the federal government itself. In fact, some precedents for aid to education were established before the federal government came into existence. While the United States still functioned under the Articles of Confederation, two laws were enacted that involved grants of aid by the national government to states for the purpose of support to schools. The aid offered by the central government through both laws came in the form of land, not money. The Land or Survey Ordinance approved by the Congress of the Confederation in 1785 established a rectangular survey system, which required that the revenue from the sale of one township be designated for the support of public education. Under the law, this was to be Section Number 16.[1]

The commonly held belief is that the Ordinance of 1787, which established the governmental unit for the Northwest Territory, reaffirmed the Land Ordinance of 1785. However, the only reference to education in the original ordinance was a general comment that education should be encouraged. The legislation that actually continued the Ordinance of 1785 was a separate act passed by the Congress two weeks after it approved the Ordinance of 1787. This particular enactment repeated the provisions for public education in the Ordinance of 1785. However, this act carried the concept of aid to education one step further by requiring the Ohio Company, which purchased that part of the territory for resales to settlers, to earmark the revenue from two townships for the support of a university. The institution that was formed under this ordinance eventually became known as Ohio State University.[2]

From the time of their passage to the present, the ordinances of

1785 and 1787 have remained the focal point of arguments about federal aid to education. Basically, an argument has developed between the proponents and opponents of federal aid concerning the intent of the Congress when it passed these ordinances. Opponents have maintained that the historical evidence indicates that Congress included these provisions as a means of encouraging settlers to buy land in the frontier territories. They contend that most of these settlers were from the Middle Atlantic and New England states where public education was considered to be important. Therefore, the argument goes, Congress was pressured by the land speculators to include such educational provisions in order to increase the marketability of the land. Proponents, on the other hand, have argued that whatever the motivation behind these provisions, the fact that they were included reflected a public concern for education and willingness by the people to accept this type of federal aid.[3]

Morrill Land-Grant Colleges Act: 1862

The next major step in the development of federal aid to education began with the election of Justin Smith Morrill to the U.S. House of Representatives in 1854. Morrill was a successful businessman and farmer from Vermont, and like a number of his contemporaries, he was deeply concerned about the future of higher education. During his nearly forty-four years of service in the House and the Senate, this concern was expressed through his sponsorship and support of several bills to aid education.[4]

Morrill's first attempt at educational legislation came in 1857 when he introduced a bill to donate federally held public lands to the states. A provision of this bill required that each state which received revenue from the sale of such lands establish at least one college in which the main course of instruction would be agricultural and mechanical arts. Under the bill, the states, including those that no longer had public lands within their borders, would receive script for lands in the western states and territories. The opposition argued that such a bill was unconstitutional on several grounds. However, in 1859, the bill was approved by a narrow margin in Congress and sent to the desk of President James Buchanan, who, however, vetoed it and cited the alleged unconstitutionality of the act. However, the item that appears to have most upset Buchanan and the opposition was the provision which required the money to be used for education. They charged that this was an attempt by the federal government to wrest control of education away from the state and local authorities. In addition, the western states charged that the bill offered an opportunity for land speculation which would disrupt the economy of the West.[5]

Morrill was not discouraged, and he introduced his bill again in the next Congress, the Thirty-seventh, which had to deal not only with a terrible Civil War but also with two important measures that concerned the public lands. After much debate, the Congress passed the Homestead Act in May 1862. The passage of this act was a victory for the agrarian reformers and probably helped smooth the way for the passage of the Morrill Act six weeks later. President Abraham Lincoln signed both acts into law. The Morrill Act as passed gave each state land-script in the amount of thirty thousand acres for each senator and resspresentative it had in Congress. The Morrill Act also required that the revenue acquired from the sale of this script be used only for those purposes stated in the act. The act required the revenue to be held in a trust by the state and the interest to be used to endow at least one college of agricultural and mechanical arts. In 1861, Morrill added a new provision to the bill as a means of increasing congressional support for it. As a result, the bill as enacted required the teaching of military tactics to the students enrolled in the colleges established under the act. Thus the Reserve Officer Training Corps (ROTC) was introduced to the land-grant colleges. The land-grant colleges had the greatest impact and importance in the western states—the region that offered the most opposition to the passage of the bill.[6]

Morrill Act: 1890

By 1872, Morrill, realizing that the colleges established under the act of 1862 needed additional federal aid, began an effort to secure the passage of a new bill that would provide additional assistance to the land-grant colleges. Finally, in August 1890, he was successful and the Second Morrill Act was passed. This act provided that each state which participated under the original act of 1862 would receive a grant of $15,000, which would increase by $1,000 per year for ten years. At the end of that period the grant would become an annual grant-in-aid of $25,000. The act also specified which particular subjects could be financed with federal funds and also required that an annual report be made by the states on how the money was spent. This act was the first federal grant that allowed a federal official to withhold funds if he felt the requirements were not being met. The result was that many land-grant colleges were able to continue as institutions of higher education. Some of them had been in dire financial conditions. The act also gave these colleges a clearer definition of the emphasis and thrust of their curriculum. Under this act it was plainly stated that the emphasis would be on professional, vocational, and scientific programs.[7]

Nelson Amendment: 1907

After the turn of the century, the land-grant colleges became increasingly concerned with their growing need for funds. By 1900 the states, under the second Morrill Act, each received a grant of $25,000. The colleges themselves wanted this amount increased. Senator Knute Nelson of Minnesota introduced a bill in late 1906 that would double the yearly grant and would allow the colleges to use some of the federal funds to train teachers in the fields of agricultural and mechanical arts. To expedite its enactment and to circumvent the opposition, Nelson attached his bill as an amendment to the agriculture appropriations bill. After a lengthy and spirited debate, the amendment was accepted and the appropriations bill passed in early March, 1907—three months after Nelson first proposed his bill. Thus, this amendment increased the grant under the Morrill act to $50,000 per year and paved the way for the use of federal funds to train teachers in vocational subjects. Although the opposition to the proposal was serious, the speed with which Nelson's amendment was accepted would seem to indicate a growing popularity of the land-grant colleges with the public as well as with their legislative representatives in Congress. Also, the interest expressed by these colleges in training vocational teachers has been viewed as an indication of the concern of the colleges for vocational education in the secondary schools.[8]

Office of Education: 1867

In the 1860s another dream of educators came to fruition. In the late 1830s, Henry Barnard—secretary of the Connecticut State Board of Education—urged the establishment of some federal offices whose duties were to include the collection and dissemination of information that pertained to education in the various states. Other educators and educational associations echoed his call throughout the 1840s and 1850s, and at the end of the Civil War, Congress again was urged to consider the matter. Ignatius Donnelly, representative from Minnesota, offered a resolution in December 1865 that called for an investigation into the need for a federal Bureau of Education. His resolution was adopted, and in February 1866, the National Association of State and City School Superintendents appointed a committee to encourage Congress to establish a Bureau of Education. This committee prepared a draft of a bill to create such a bureau. James A. Garfield, representative from Ohio and later president of the United States, agreed to present the bill to Congress. After a lengthy period of consideration, Garfield managed to get the bill approved by the House. The Senate passed the bill on March 1, 1867, and President Andrew Johnson signed it the following day. Several days later, President Johnson appointed Henry Barnard as the first commissioner of education.[9]

This act created the Department of Education, an independent agency without cabinet rank. It was headed by a commissioner rather than a secretary. The new department's duties were to collect and distribute data on the conditions, problems, and accomplishments of education in the nation, and, it was made responsible for the administration of the Morrill Act. Later, the department was charged with the responsibility of overseeing the education of the Eskimo in Alaska.[10]

Almost immediately after its creation, the department ran into difficulty. In 1869 it lost its independent status and was relegated to the position of a bureau within the Department of Interior, were it existed for several years in a hostile environment as the higher administrators within the Department of Interior considered it to be unnecessary and unwanted. Nevertheless, the bureau diligently went about its work and its relations with the rest of the department improved. By 1886 the bureau staff had grown in number from two to thirty-eight. This improvement of interdepartmental relations and the increase in staff was primarily the result of the effectiveness and tenure of the second commissioner of the bureau—John Eaton. The bureau continued to be a part of the Department of Interior until it was transferred to the Federal Security Agency in 1939 and renamed the Office of Education. Then in 1953 it became a part of the newly created HEW—Department of Health, Education, and Welfare.[11]

Hatch Act: 1887

In the period that followed the enactment of the Morrill

Land-Grant College Act, various individuals and groups which represented agriculture began to call for the establishment of experimental stations to do research in agriculture. Throughout the 1870s and early 1880s, the movement to establish agricultural experimental stations grew. The general feeling among those involved seemed to be that the federal government should initiate and/or support these stations. A bill was drafted in 1882 that called for the establishment of experimental stations connected to the land-grant colleges but controlled by the Department of Agriculture. State government, education groups, and the land-grant colleges opposed the bill because none of them would have control of the stations. Finally, a new bill that met with the approval of those concerned was passed by Congress in 1887. This legislation became known as the Hatch Act because of the effort of one of its sponsors—Representative William Henry Hatch of Missouri.[12]

The Hatch Act provided an annual grant of $15,000 to each state to fund agricultural experimental stations that were to be directed by the land-grant colleges. The act also stipulated that the funds would come from the sale of public lands. However, the origin of the funding was soon changed and attached directly to the Agriculture Department's appropriations. The Hatch Act also specified certain conditions and regulations that concerned the expenditure and control of the grants. The grants were to be used to conduct research and experimentation into matters that concerned agriculture, e.g., production methods, new breeds of livestock, new types of crops, plant and animal diseases, and any other concerns which bore directly on American agriculture. The act also required that personnel assigned to the stations could not be used by the land-grant colleges as instructors during the hours normally assigned for station use. Theoretically, the grants were not to be used to provide teaching staff for the land-grant colleges. However, there is some historical indication that a number of the colleges circumvented this restriction and used station staff as instructors. The act gave the Department of Agriculture certain rights and powers concerning the withholding of funds, periodical inspections, and general advisory and supervisory functions. A final stipulation in the act was that each station was required to submit an annual report of its activities and expenses to the governor of its state or territory. The experimental stations created by the Hatch Act were instrumental features in the revolution that came to American agriculture. Through the research conducted by these stations, the quantity and quality of agricultural production improved greatly. As a result, the American farmer came to recognize the value of research as well as vocational education.[13]

Adams Act: 1906

In March 1906, the Adams Act was approved by Congress. This law increased the grant for agricultural experimental stations by $5,000 the first year and by $2,000 a year for the following five years. As a result, the yearly grant for experimental stations was increased to $30,000 by 1911—double the amount provided by the Hatch Act.[14]

With the passage of the Adams Act, federal aid to education had completed a basic change. In the beginning, in the 1780s, federal aid to education was tied to the land when the federal government gave land to the states for educational purposes. Gradually this changed and the grants became funds derived from the sale of lands. In 1900, a provision was made that allowed U.S. Treasury funds to be used if land sales were not sufficient to cover the amount needed for the yearly grants. The Adams Act required grants to the experimental stations to come from any surplus in the Treasury—thus entirely removing the grants from land and land sales. With the Adams Act, the concept of direct federal payments to the states for vocational purposes was acceptable enough to get it through the Congress and the executive branch.[15]

As the source of the grants changed from public lands to federal revenue, the purposes and uses of the grants also changed. The relationship between the federal government and the states concerning the grants was altered significantly. Slowly the relationship evolved from the grant of a gift into a contractual arrangement between the parties, with the federal government reserving the right to either increase or discontinue the grants. Also during the period of 1785 to 1906, the federal government developed certain discretionary powers over the grants. Requirements as to how the funds were to be used, what subjects could be taught with federal money, and the filing of annual reports were placed upon the states. Another important part of the evolution in the overall purpose of federal grants occurred before 1906. The original grants were to be used for the advancement of general education. By 1906, the federal government provided funds for specific types of education—primarily vocational education. To this end, the land-grant colleges made a major contribution. Through the establishment of vocational agriculture high schools, the development of short courses on particular vocational topics, and the creation of the extension services, the land-grant colleges provided needed vocational services to those they served, and they demonstrated to the public the value that could come from the use of federal funds.[16]

Federal Involvement at the Turn of the Century

As the twentieth century opened, the federal government found itself firmly established as a participant in the educational scheme of the nation. Through the use of grants-in-aid, a federal policy of education evolved that emphasized the practical rather than the general—the vocational and professional over the liberal arts and humanities. Through the land-grant colleges and the experimental agricultural stations, the federal government actively encouraged the development of scientific research. However, it required the research to be slanted to the practical side and to be aimed at finding ways to improve either agricultural or industrial production. Because of its emphasis on practical subjects and practical research, the federal policy at the turn of the century stressed the education of the masses rather than that of a more elite group of students. This was the goal of its grants— vocational education for the improved well-being of the general populace. However at the turn of the century, the grants of federal funds were still aimed at the adult worker. The land-grant colleges and the experimental stations were intended to train young adults for careers in agriculture or the mechanical arts and to develop ways of improving the production methods of those already active in these careers. Federal policy and grants had not been extended below the collegiate level. Nevertheless, during the early years of the twentieth century the necessary precedents were established and the basic needs were defined for the extension of federal aid into the secondary schools. The stage was set, and the opportunity for such aid was nearer than ever before in American life.[17]

Growth of Support for Federal Aid to Vocational Education

National Society for Promotion of Industrial Education

One twentieth-century organization that was most adamant in its support for federal aid to vocational education was the National Society for the Promotion of Industrial Education. This organization was founded through the efforts of Charles R. Richards, professor of manual training at Columbia University, and James P. Haney, director of art and manual training in the New York City school system. Richards recognized the need for a national organization that would support industrial education. At first, he thought the way to achieve this was to obtain the support of established organizations of national scope. The logical groups whose support would be of the most value were educational organizations. When he approached these educational groups, Richards found them to be either apathetic, preoccupied with other interests, or financially unable to get involved. Richards realized that a new organization was needed to support industrial education. In the summer of 1906, he joined with James P. Haney in calling for a meeting of those with a deep concern for the future of industrial education. This original meeting was attended by thirteen men. By November, interest in the project had grown and the organizational meeting of the group was attended by two hundred and fifty people from twenty states. At this meeting on November 16, 1906, the National Society for the Promotion of Industrial Education was created. An important feature of the organizational meeting was that those who attended represented business and industry as well as professional educators. Thus, from the beginning, the society drew support from both sides interested in the advancement of industrial education.[18]

Within one year after its creation, the society reported that it had some type of statewide organization in thirty-five states. The strength of the society, however, was concentrated in the East—primarily along the Atlantic seaboard. During the first decade of its existence, the society promoted industrial education through national conventions, study committees, reports, and society bulletins. In 1910 the society also sponsored a lecture tour of the United States by Dr. George Kerschensteiner, the director of Education in Munich, Germany. Kerschensteiner had developed a system of continuation schools—industrial and vocational education—in Munich that was internationally known and respected. His speeches, which compared German and American industrial education, did much to increase the interest of Americans in industrial education. The comparison of industrial education in America and Germany left many Americans with a sense of inferiority and a zealous desire to catch and surpass the Germans. Through Kerschensteiner's, speeches, the society was able to create considerable political support for industrial education on a nationwide basis. One of the most dramatic changes that historically has been attributed to Kerschensteiner's visit was the shift of position by the National Association of Manufacturers. Within a one-year period, the NAM dropped its long-time support for trade schools and became a very active adherent to the concept of the continuation schools.[19]

Although from its beginning the society had promoted state and federal legislation for vocational education, a change in its program occurred in 1912, when Dr. Charles A. Prosser became the secretary of the society. With his assumption of the post, the society's active movement for federal aid to vocational education began in earnest. In 1914 the work of the society became an important factor in the creation of the national commission on federal aid to vocational education.[20]

In 1918, the society changed its name to the National Society for Vocational Education, thus giving official recognition to its interest in types of vocational training other than industrial education. In addition, the society, by 1918, was not the only broad-based organization interested in vocational education. In 1914, a group had met at Chicago and organized the Vocational Education Association (VEA), which was created because of the society's concentration on the eastern seaboard. The Midwest felt that the society did not fully represent its needs. Therefore, the VEA tended to be an organization that represented Midwest interests and opinions. Within a few years, the VEA was nearly as large and as influential as the National Society for Vocational Education. In 1926, the Vocational Education Association and the National Society for Vocational Education merged to form the organization that today is known as the American Vocational Association (AVA).[21]

Agricultural Agencies

A major source of pressure on the local, state, and national levels for vocational education was the agricultural organizations. A number of these groups had been actively agitating for practical education for as long or longer than had those interested in industrial education. Such organizations as the National Grange, the Association of American Agricultural Colleges and Experiment Stations, the Farmer's Union, the American Society of Equity, and such agricultural publications as *Wallace's Farmer* and *Hoard's Dairyman* actively worked for a reform of education that would include vocational agriculture in the secondary schools and/or the colleges. In 1874 the National Grange stated its interest in the teaching of practical agriculture and those sciences necessary to the rural-farm life. The Association of American Agricultural Colleges and Experiment Stations was influential in the passage of federal legislation that concerned the land-grant colleges, the experimental stations, and extension services. By the opening years of the twentieth century these agricultural organizations reflected a strong rural-farm demand for vocational education. If the forces of these agricultural groups were joined with those interested in industrial training, many observers thought that the pressure exerted on political institutions could be immense. And such a union of efforts for Vocational Education did come about during the twentieth century.[22]

National Education Association

At the turn of the century, the National Education Association (NEA) was probably the most prestigious educational organization in the United States. Early in the century it expressed its interest in vocational education through discussion groups (at the 1900 and 1901 annual meetings) and special study reports on industrial education (1905, 1907, and 1908). The NEA continued to issue reports on vocational education and to make recommendations concerning the vocational needs of the nation. All of its reports and recommendations notwithstanding, the NEA was not an aggressive promoter of vocational education, and it was not in the forefront of the effort to improve vocational education. In fact, the NEA opposed some of the early bills for federal aid to vocational education, apparently, in part, because it was not consulted when the bills were drafted. Also, a split within the membership concerning the place of vocational training in the general scheme of education played a significant part in keeping the NEA from any leadership position. In fact, the division within the NEA reached the point that those in vocational education abandoned the NEA, and its Department of Vocational Education all but ceased to function after the late 1920s.[23]

American Federation of Labor

The attitude of organized labor was a critical factor for vocational education. Historically, whereas legislation concerning vocational education might be passed without the support of labor, the success of such vocational training usually depended upon labor. If labor would not accept the vocational graduates into the crafts and trades, the system was doomed. The posture of labor toward vocational education varied between the organizations representing labor—some actively supported it, some vigorously opposed it, and others simply ignored it.[24]

The attitudes of the American Federation of Labor (AFL)— the largest labor organization at the turn of the century—were especially significant. In the nineteenth century, the AFL was an active advocate of educational reform and compulsory education. However, its attitude in the twentieth century toward vocational education was mixed. The AFL supported the concept of vocational training in the public schools, but only as a supplement to the general curriculum. The AFL was opposed to the dualistic system that had developed in some states where general education and vocational education were two distinct systems. The AFL supported vocational education but vigorously opposed any administrative organization that did not include representatives from labor on the policymaking boards or which gave control of the boards to the representatives of management. It supported the concept of publicly financed vocational education, but condemned trade schools—both public and private. The AFL believed that they were poorly managed, controlled by the employers, and produced an inferior worker. It viewed the trade schools as a means that allowed management to maintain a surplus of labor and thus keep wages down. The AFL also supported federal legislation and federal aid for vocational education— provided that it met the AFL's criteria. Although none of the proposals which faced the Congress met all of the AFL's requirements, it did give its support to many of the vocational bills during the first decades of this century.[25]

National Association of Manufacturers

Among the groups that represented management, the National Association of Manufacturers (NAM) stood in the forefront. The NAM supported trade and technical schools in the late nineteenth century, and it viewed these schools as a source for skilled workers. This was directly opposite the view of labor that held them to be a source of cheap labor, company men, and strikebreakers. During the first decade of the twentieth century, the NAM came to look with favor on vocational education through continuation schools. It supported the concept of practical education and was skeptical about the ability of professional educators to administer such a program. The NAM maintained that vocational education should be under a separate system and administered by a board that represented workers, farmers, and employers. Through the statements of some of its leaders, the NAM made it clear that by "workers" they did not necessarily mean the unions. The NAM maintained that organized labor did not have a rightful place in education. Whereas the NAM was generally supportive of vocational education and was receptive to the concept of federal aid, it tended to base its support or its opposition to proposed legislation primarily upon the composition of the administrative boards and those who controlled them. To get and to keep the support of both labor and management for specific bills required much work by those educational reformers who guided the proposals through Congress.[26]

Chamber of Commerce

Another group that reflected the sentiment of an important segment of American society was the Chamber of Commerce of the United States. This is a wholly twentieth-century body organized in 1912. The chamber established its natural policies by a poll of its members. When an important issue arose, the chamber conducted a referendum. It sent ballots to each of its member chapters, which voted either for or against the issue and cast a number of votes prescribed by a formula based on the membership of the chapter. Under the formula, each chapter cast between a minimum of one to a maximum of ten votes. When the ballots were returned, the Chamber of Commerce tabulated the votes and the opinion expressed by the membership through the ballots became the official policy of the chamber. Moreover, it would remain the policy until changed by another referendum. At the first annual convention of the chamber held in 1913, the delegates endorsed the concepts of vocational education in the areas of industry, business, agriculture, and home economics. The delegates also approved the use of federal funds to support such vocational training. After the chamber's Committee on Education issued its report on federal aid to vocational education, the chamber conducted a referendum in the spring of 1916. Four issues were on the ballot: (1) the use of liberal federal aid for vocational education, (2) a uniform allotment of federal aid among the states, (3) appointment of a paid professional board to oversee the use of the funds, and (4) the appointment of advisory boards representing all interested factions to make recommendations to the federal board. In each case, over 80 percent of the ballots favored the item. Thus, in 1916 the chamber officially supported federal aid to vocational education.[27]

Theodore Roosevelt and the Progressive Spirit

The first two decades of the twentieth century constitute a time that is termed by historians as the Progressive Era. Basically, Progressivism was a political and social reform movement, which called for the return of political power to the people. To do this, the Progressives worked to obtain the direct election of United States Senators, direct primary elections, initiative, referendum, and recall. Once the people regained the reins of government from the corrupt, the rich, and the bosses, the Progressives firmly believed that the people would use their power for the betterment of the many, rather than for the good of the few. In this way, the nation would be stengthened politically, socially, and economically. When proposals to improve vocational training were introduced into this environment, many Progressives could see the connection between vocational education and the improvement of American life. One Progressive who recognized the value of vocational training was the energetic man who became one of the leading symbols of the era—President Theodore Roosevelt.

In 1907, the National Society for the Promotion of Industrial Education contacted some three hundred persons of importance in government, education, management, and labor and requested their views concerning industrial education. One of those who responded at length was Theodore Roosevelt. His vigorous response covered not only industrial training but all of vocational education. Roosevelt exalted the work ethic and the workingman. It was his wholehearted belief that those in agriculture, crafts, industry, and home economics were just as professional and worthy of quality training as engineers, physicians, and attorneys. Roosevelt also believed that with such training each individual could function as an efficient economic unit. If such an individual could do quality work and support himself and his family, the nation unquestionably would be strengthened. The National Society widely publicized the results of its survey through a bulletin and reprinted Roosevelt's letter as in introduction to the material. This was not Roosevelt's first public statement favoring vocational education. The preceeding December he had devoted part of his annual message to the Congress to the topic of vocational education. In his message Roosevelt commented that he hoped the Interstate Commerce clause might be used as a means of getting federal assistance for vocational education.[28]

First Bills

Pollard Bill: 1906

Congress was not idle in the years between the turn of the century and the passage of the Smith-Hughes Act in 1917. During those seventeen years, several pieces of legislation were introduced that sought to improve vocational education. One of the first important attempts to approve federal and for vocational education was the Pollard Bill of 1906. This proposal, also known as the Burkett-Pollard Bill, was introduced into the House by Representative Ernest M. Pollard of Nebraska and into the Senate by Senator Elmer J. Burkett of Nebraska. The bill called for federal appropriations to state normal schools for the training of secondary teachers of agriculture, mechanical arts, home economics, and other areas. Under this proposal, a maximum of $1 million per year would be appropriated for this purpose. One-half of the funds was to be divided equally among the states, whereas the remainder was to be divided among the normal schools according to length of service and enrollment. While this bill was before Congress from 1906 to 1911, it received support from the National Education Association and organizations that represented the normal schools. The failure to approve the bill probably was caused by the opposition of the Association of American Agricultural Colleges and Experiment Stations. This group believed that the land-grant colleges rather than the normal schools should train teachers of agriculture and mechanical arts. At its annual meeting in the autumn after the introduction of the Pollard Bill, the Association authorized the drafting of a proposal that would provide some federal funds and would give the land-grant colleges control of teacher education in these areas. This proposal ultimately became the Nelson Amendment of 1907. Although the Pollard Bill lingered on in the Congress until 1911, the Association and the Nelson Amendment effectively killed it in 1907.[29]

Livingston Bill: 1906

Interest in vocational education was also strong in the South. One of the southern states that led in the vocational movement was Georgia. In 1906, Representative Leonidas Livingston of Georgia followed the request of the state legislature and introduced into Congress a bill that called for the establishment of an agricultural secondary school in each congressional distinct in the nation with an annual federal appropriation of $10,000 for each school established. Thus, the South issued the first call for the extension of federal aid for agricultural education into the secondary schools. The bill, however, failed to gain congressional approval.[30]

Davis Bill: 1907

Representative Charles R. Davis of Minnesota combined the concepts of the Livingston Bill with other bills before Congress, added some ideas of his own, and presented it to the House in 1907. Davis proposed that federal funds be appropriated and distributed to rural high schools for instruction in agriculture and home economics. He also requested that federal funds be allocated to urban secondary school for the teaching of mechnical arts and home economics. The bill placed the administration of the act in the hands of the secretary of agriculture.[31]

The Davis Bill met immediate opposition from the U. S. commissioner of education, the National Education Association, and the National Society for the Promotion of Industrial Education. The society refused to support the bill because it thought that it was hastily drafted. The society called for an extensive study to be made of the nation's vocational needs before any legislation was approved. The NEA and the Commissioner also cited the need for a study as a reason for their opposition. However, the fact that the NEA was not consulted during the drafting of the bill and that the administration of the act would be under the Department of Agriculture almost certainly were important reasons for their opposition. However, the bill was not without its supporters. The National Grange, the Farmers' National Congress, the State of Georgia, and the Southern Educational Association all endorsed the bill. In an effort to appease the opposition, the bill was revised and amended several times between 1907 and 1910. However, the efforts of the bill's supporters failed and the opposition held firm.[32]

Dolliver-Davis Bill: 1910

In 1910, the American Federation of Labor endorsed the principle of federal aid to vocational education but withheld its support from the Davis Bill. It referred the Davis Bill to its committee on industrial education that recommended further changes in the bill. This revised draft was given to Senator Jonathan P. Dolliver of Iowa. In January 1910, Senator Dolliver presented this revision to the Senate and Representative Davis introduced it into the House. The Dolliver-Davis Bill changed the federal payments to the states from a per-capita basis to a lump sum payment. It also shifted the administration of the act from the secretary of agriculture to the Department of Interior. In June 1910, the Senate Committee on Agriculture and Forestry combined the Dolliver-Davis Bill with another bill by Representative J. C. McLaughin of Michigan. The McLaughin Bill called for additional appropriations to expand the extension work of the landgrant colleges. It was hoped that the combination of these bills would provide the various opposition groups with some feature they could support. Several groups including the American Federation of Labor did give their support to the bill. However, the National Society for the Promotion of Industrial Education remained adamant in its opposition and continued to call for a study of the national needs before endorsing any legislation. The society supported the concept of federal aid but continued its opposition to the generalities and inadequacies it found in the Dolliver-Davis Bill. With the death of Senator Dolliver in October 1910, the supporters of the bill turned their attention to another piece of pending legislation—the Page Bill.[33]

Page Bills: 1911–1912

With the death of Senator Dolliver, interest turned to the proposal of Senator Carroll S. Page of Vermont. In the spring of 1911, Senator Page introduced a bill that called for an annual appropriation of $5 million for vocational instruction in the public secondary schools, $4 million for support of state-controlled agricultural high schools, $1 million for agricultural experiment stations at the state controlled schools, and a $1 million appropriation for the normal schools to train vocational teachers, and additional sums for the continuation of the extension work of the land-grant colleges and agricultural experiment stations. The act was to be administered by the secretary of the interior in consultation with the Departments of Commerce, Labor, and Agriculture.[34]

The Page Bill was revised several times during the next two years. Although the bill was able to gain the support of such diverse groups as the American Federation of Labor, the National Association of Manfacturers, the National Grange, the Farmers' Union, and the National Society for the Promotion of Industrial Education, the opposition was steadfast and congressional approval was denied. The opposition made several charges against the bill including a question of constitutionality. The wisdom of placing the responsibility for the training of vocational teachers with the normal schools rather than the land-grant colleges was questioned. The necessity of creating a new system of agricultural schools and agricultural experiment stations was debated. However, a major source of irritation to a large portion of the opposition was the attempt to place appropriations for established agricultural activities in the same legislation creating a new vocational program. In fact, a bill was introduced that concerned the appropriations for agricultural extension work. This bill, the Smith-Level Bill, was an effective block to the attempts to pass the Page Bill. An argument even evolved concerning whether or not agricultural extension matters and vocational education should be considered in one bill or in separate acts, and if they should be in separate bills, which should get first consideration for passage. The result was a legislative deadlock.[35]

Commission on National Aid to Vocational Education

Compromise over Smith-Lever

After much debate and revision, the final draft of the Smith-Lever Bill called for the expansion of the agricultural extension work with the federal and state governments sharing the cost. The bill allocated a federal appropriation of $600,000 for the first year to be increased in each of the seven following years by $500,000 per year. When this period ended, the federal appropriations would stabilize at $4.1 million per year. This money was to be disbursed to the states on the basis of their rural population. An important feature of the act was that such state was required to match from its own treasury all federal funds received in excess of $10,000. After much effort and compromise, the Smith-Lever

Act became law in May 1914.[36]

The legislative deadlock between the Page Bill and the Smith-Lever Bill was broken primarily through the efforts of the National Society for the Promotion of Industrial Education and Senator Hoke Smith of Georgia—the Senate sponsor of the Smith-Lever Bill. Senator Smith had supported vocational education for a number of years, and the society did not oppose the concept of agricultural extension work. After some consultation, it was agreed that the society would end its pressure for passage of the Page Bill, which would make it possible for the agricultural interests to push for the approval of the Smith-Lever Bill. In return, Senator Smith promised to introduce and support a resolution calling for the establishment of a commission to investigate national aid to vocational education. In accordance with this agreement, the Senate approved the Smith-Lever Bill and the following day Senator Smith introduced the resolution into the Senate. The debate was brief and the resolution was passed rather quickly. It was approved by the president on January 20, 1914.[37]

Commission on National Aid to Vocational Education

The enabling resolution required the commission to be a bipartisan body appointed by the president. According to political affiliation, the commission was constituted in the prescribed manner. The commission, however, did have one outstanding bias—all its members were dedicated to the concept of federal aid for vocational education. In fact, the lay members of the commission—the appointed representatives of various organizations—were all members of the National Society for the Promotion of Industrial Education. The congressional portion of the commission consisted of Senators Hoke Smith and Carroll S. Page and Representatives Simeon D. Fess of Ohio and Dudley M. Hughes of Georgia. The other members of the commission were John A. Lepp, secretary of the Indiana Commission on Industrial and Agricultural Education; Florence M. Marshall, director, Manhattan Trade School for Girls; Agnes Nestor, president, International Glove Workers' Union; Charles A. Prosser, secretary, National Society for the Promotion of Industrial Education; and Charles H. Winslow, special agent, Bureau of Labor Statistics, and member of the Douglas Commission in Massachusetts, 1906–1909. The enabling resolution required the commission to complete its work by June 1, 1914. The organizational meeting of the commission was held in early April. Senator Smith was elected chairman, a staff of forty-five was employed, and work began.[38]

After its first meeting, the commission had less than sixty days to complete its work. There were no shirkers on the commission. Although not all of the members could attend every meeting, the commission was in session nearly every day through April and May. It examined documents, analyzed statistics, held hearings, conducted a survey, and issued a two-volume report including recommendations and a legislative proposal. Not only did the commission complete its assignment on time, it also did the work at less cost than anticipated; the commission returned to the treasury one-third of the funds allotted for its expenses.[39]

From its beginning there was no doubt that the commission would find in favor of federal aid to vocational education. It was just a matter of determining what types of vocational education were eligible and how much aid should be given. The commission decided to examine six areas concerning federal aid and vocational education. These were (1) the need for vocational education in the United States, (2) the need for federal aid to vocational education, (3) the types of vocational education that should receive federal funds, (4) the use of federal agencies in providing aid to vocational education, (5) the extent of federal aid, and (6) the conditions under which federal aid should be given.[40]

When its work was completed, the commission recommended in its report that federal aid be used to stimulate vocational training in agriculture, trades, and industry. It suggested that the federal funds be used to train teachers in agricultural, trade, and industrial subjects, and home economics. It also urged that a portion of the federal aid be used to pay part of the salaries of those engaged in the teaching and administration of vocational education. The commission recommended that federal aid should go to those schools that were supported and controlled by the public, were of less than college grade level, and were designed to prepare boys and girls over fourteen years of age for a vocation. Three types of schools should be eligible for the aid—all-day schools, part-time schools, and evening schools. The commission proposed that a Federal Board for Vocational Education be established to administer the program at the national level. On the state level, the commission recommended a state board be organized to supervise vocational education within the state. The commission believed that certain conditions should be established governing the use of federal funds. Foremost among these were (1) a federal statute be written concerning the responsibility of the states in safeguarding and effectively using the federal funds,

(2) the states through their legislative bodies formally accept this federal law, (3) the state board with the approval of the Federal Board establish standards concerning administration of funds, equipment, and teacher qualifications, and (4) the states match from their own funds all federal money used in training teachers and paying salaries of teachers and administrators. The commission also drafted a bill that embodied these recommendations. This proposed legislation was turned over to the Senate and House Committees on Education that were chaired by Senator Smith and Representative Hughes. Senator Smith introduced the bill into the Senate in December 1915 and Congressman Hughes introduced it in the House shortly thereafter.[41]

The Smith-Hughes Bill

The Sponsors

The Georgians, Hoke Smith and Dudley M. Hughes, were longtime supporters of vocational education. Smith had had little formal education and his instruction was primarily what his father, a history professor at the University of North Carolina, taught him at home. Smith was admitted to the bar and practiced law in Atlanta. In 1887 he bought the *Atlanta Evening Journal* and served as its editor and publisher until 1900. Smith became active in politics during the last decade of the nineteenth century. He served in the administration of President Grover Cleveland as secretary of the interior, 1893–1896. He was governor of Georgia on two occasions—1907–1909 and again briefly in 1911. As governor, Smith was an advocate of vocational education. From 1911 to 1921 he was United States senator from Georgia.[42]

Dudley M. Hughes attended the University of Georgia, but did not graduate. In 1870, he started his farming operations and remained heavily involved in farming throughout his life. He was a member of the original group that planned and built the Macon, Dublin, and Savannah Railroad. He also served as president of the company and was a member of the board of directors. At various times, he was a member of the boards of trustees of the State Normal Institute (Danville), of the Georgia Institute of Technology (Atlanta), and of the University of Georgia (Athens). He served one term in the state senate—1882–1883—and four terms in the United States Houses of Representatives—1909–1917.[43]

Passage of the Smith-Hughes Act: 1917

The eighteen months between the time the commission submitted its report and the introduction of the commission's recommendations via the Smith-Hughes Bill were not the result of procrastination by the sponsors of the legislation. Senator Smith defended the delay by pointing out that the proponents of vocational education used the interim period to publicize the commission and its recommendations. The two-volume report of the commission was published in 1914 by the Government Printing Office and was widely distributed. Also, the National Society for the Promotion of Industrial Education used the eighteen months to promote support for the commission's recommendations in each of the states where the society was active. The philosophy seemed to be one involving an effort to educate the public concerning the recommendations rather than a hurried attempt to gain quick passage of the proposed bill. Whereas some were frustrated by the nearly three years that it took to get the recommendations into law, Senator Smith cited the small amount of criticism directed toward the proposal, the limited efforts to amend it, and the enthusiasm with which the public accepted it as evidence that the delay was worthwhile.[44]

When the bill was introduced into the Congress, the political situation was such that it would be over a year before much action would be taken. The bill had the support of the majority in both the House and the Senate. In fact, support in the Senate was such that no senator actively opposed the bill. However, other matters such as the war in Europe and the coming general elections pushed the bill into the background. The bill was amended in both the House and the Senate. One of the more important changes came in the House when the co-sponsor, Dudley M. Hughes, improved the portion on home economics and tried to equalize it with agriculture, trades, and industry. The Senate passed its version of the bill in July 1916. Hughes addressed the House concerning the bill in late July and it seemed the House was ready to consider the proposal. While the noncongressional supporters of the bill waited anxiously, the bill was not brought before the House and it adjourned in September without considering the Smith-Hughes Bill. This delay was in part the result of the illness that caused Representative Hughes to be absent during most of this time. Also with the general elections coming in November, with all of the congressional seats involved, many members of the Houses were on the campaign trail in their districts. In fact, attendance in the House was so poor during August that a quorum was not present.[45]

While Congress deliberated through the spring and summer of 1916, support for federal aid to vocational education continued to grow. One important influence upon the prospects of the Smith-Hughes Bill was the survey by the United States Chamber of Commerce of its membership (cited earlier in this chapter). This survey concerned the basic concepts embodied in the Smith-Hughes Bill. The chamber reported in June that all of the items on its survey were approved by at least an 80 percent majority. Thus an important organization representing businessmen and merchants was placed firmly in support of the bill.[46]

When Congress reconvened in December 1916, President Woodrow Wilson placed special emphasis on vocational education in his message to the Congress. Wilson had supported vocational education in the past and he viewed it as an integral part of his national preparedness plan. Wilson argued that if the United States was forced to become involved in the war in Europe, vocational education would greatly strengthen the industrial and agricultural production of the nation. He urged Congress to pass the Smith-Hughes bill as soon as possible. Congress immediately set about the task of reconciling the differences between the Senate and House versions of the bill. In less than three months, the Congress debated, amended, reconciled, and passed the bill. On February 23, 1917, President Wilson signed it into law. Federal aid to vocational education on the secondary level was then a reality.[47]

Although many organizations were active in the struggle to obtain federal aid for vocational education, the role of the National Society for the Promotion of Industrial Education in this effort cannot be passed over lightly. The Society was the most vocal and the most dedicated of the groups. Its constant efforts to promote vocational education and its repetitive calls for in-depth studies and legislation provided a focal point around which the supporters of vocational education could rally. It had long called for a national commission to study the vocational needs of the country. And when the commission was formed, those appointed to it had close ties with the society. The society provided the major influence when the commission drafted the proposal that became the Smith-Hughes Act. And, it would be influential in the administration of the act. Whereas Senator Smith and Representative Hughes gave valuable service as midwives, the real parent of the act was the National Society for the Promotion of Industrial Education.

Provisions of the Smith-Hughes Act

The Smith-Hughes Act—Public Law 347, 64th Congress—provided for a continuing appropriation that would be distributed among the participating states. Each state would receive funds for vocational agriculture according to the proportion of the national total of rural population it had within its borders. Allocations for industrial, and trade subjects, and home economics would be made according to each state's proportion of the total national urban population. However, a guaranteed minimum allocation was provided for those states with very small rural or urban populations. Under the act, the states were required to establish and fund suitable programs and the federal appropriations would then be used to reimburse the states and their local districts for up to one-half of their expenditures in these programs. An important feature of Smith-Hughes was the requirement that the states and local districts match on a dollar-for-dollar basis any federal money they received. If the states failed to do so, the federal administration could withhold all or a portion of the next year's funds. The Smith-Hughes Act called for an initial allocation of $1,660,000 for the fiscal year ending June 30, 1918, and increasing each year until it reached $7,167,000 in 1926. This amount would then be an annual appropriation. These funds were divided into three types: (1) those used to pay the salaries of teachers, supervisors, and directors of agricultural programs; (2) those used to pay the salaries of teachers of home economics, industrial, and trade subjects; and (3) those used to train teachers, supervisors, and directors of agricultural programs and teachers of home economics, industrial, and trade subjects. The importance of the rural influence and the high priority given agriculture by Congress can be noted in that federal funds could be used to train and pay only the supervisors and the directors of agricultural programs. Persons holding similar positions in home economics, industrial, and trade programs were not eligible for federal funds.[48]

In general, the privisions of the Smith-Hughes Act concerning the types of schools, age of students, kinds of programs, and restrictions on the use of federal funds followed the major items in the recommendations of the Commission on National Aid to Vocational Education. Except for teacher training, the programs were to be less than college level and the students had to be four-teen years of age or older. Three types of schools were approved for possible federal funding: (1) full-time day schools to provide vocational training to boys and girls in areas that they desire to gain employment, (2) part-time schools for those employed but who can devote part of their time to receiving training in their field, and, (3) evening schools for those who desire additional training in their vocations but cannot arrange to attend the part-time schools. Participation under Smith-Hughes was not compulsory for the states. However, the states were required to voluntarily accept the conditions and restrictions of the act if they wanted federal aid for their vocational programs. Among these conditions were the establishment of a system of public control of the schools to receive the funds, a guarantee of the safety of the federal funds allocated to the state, an audit and report system, and the recognition that the federal government could withhold the funds if the state's programs or its administration of the programs did not meet the requirements of the Smith-Hughes Act.[49]

To oversee the administration of the federal vocational education program, the Smith-Hughes Act also created a Federal Board of Vocational Education. This board consisted of the secretaries of agriculture, commerce, and labor, the commissioner of education, and three public members appointed by the president. One of the appointed members was to be a representative of the agricultural interests, the second was to represent labor, and the third was to represent manufacturing and commerce. An annual appropriation of $200,000 was allocated for the administration of the Smith-Hughes Act.[50]

The Federal Board for Vocational Education

Organization of the Board

President Wilson signed the Smith-Hughes Act on February 23, 1917. By the end of the following July, the Federal Board of Vocational Education was organized and beginning to function. The first board consisted of David F. Houston, secretary of agriculture; William C. Redfield, secretary of commerce; William B. Wilson, secretary of labor; and Philander P. Claxton, commissioner of education. The three members appointed by the president and approved by the Senate were Arthur E. Holder of Iowa, representing labor; Charles A. Greathouse of Indiana, representing agriculture; and James P. Munroe of Massachusetts, representing the commercial and manufacturing interests. One of the first items of business for the board was the appointment of its chief executive officer. This position was to be known as the federal director of Vocational Education. The board unanimously agreed to appoint Charles A. Prosser to this position. Prosser, whose activities have been noted previously, was an excellent choice. He was well known and respected in his field, he was dedicated to vocational education, and he was an excellent organizer. The board also appointed assistant directors for each of the major vocational areas assigned to the board—agricultural education, trade and industrial education, home economics education, and research services. Later, an assistant director for commercial education was appointed. In order to facilitate the supervision and administration of the federal aid, the board also divided the nation into five regions. Each region would have a special agent from each of the appropriate divisions—usually agriculture and trades and industries. These agents operated out of a major city in the region selected for its central location and ease of transportation. These regional divisions and their headquarter cities were (1) North Atlantic Region—New York City, (2) Southern Region—Atlanta, (3) North Central Region—Indianapolis, (4) West Central Region—Kansas City, Missouri, and (5) Pacific Region—San Francisco.[51]

Establishment of Policies

One of the first problems facing the newly organized board was the establishment of policies that would govern their operations and decisions. The board quickly drafted a series of temporary policies, which were published in November, 1917 in a bulletin known as a *Statement of Policies, Bulletin No. 1*. Although these were intended to be only temporary policies, the board found that most of the temporary policies were quite workable as permanent statements of policy. Although the board revised and reissued its policy statement on several occasions during its existence, the major permanent policies remained essentially the same as the temporary ones drafted in 1917.[52]

What may have been the board's most statement of policy was made in early September 1917. A question was submitted to the board asking whether or not federal money for vocational education could be spent to establish programs for those mentally and emotionally deficient, those with deviant behavior patterns, and others viewed as troublesome in traditional classroom activities. The board's answer was absolutely and unequivocally no. Therefore, from its beginning, the board held that federal funds under the Smith-Hughes Act were to be used to create quality vocational training. The vocational programs were not to be used as a means of removing from the traditional curriculum those who could not function or who caused disruptions. Vocational education was to be an equal to the traditional programs. It was not to be a holding pen for the castoffs of the traditional curriculum.[53]

The body of the board's policies concerned the administration of the Smith-Hughes Act and the interpretation and implimentation of those provisions of the act that were not clearly stated or that were left to the judgment of the Board. Into this latter group fell such questions as what was an hour of instruction. Was it one class period that may vary considerably in length from school to school? Or, was it one clock hour of sixty minutes? Numerous decisions of this type faced the board as it made an effort to standardize the basic factors concerning vocational education. However, at the heart of the board's statement of policies were the four precepts that guided the board. These basic principles reflected the philosophical arguments that had supported the call for federal aid during the preceding years. First, the function of the Federal Board for Vocational Education and the federal funds it administered was to stimulate the states into providing vocational education programs that would in turn strengthen the nation. Second, the board through the use of the federal funds would equalize the financial burden involved in providing vocational education. Third, through the use of federal funds, the national government would become a member of the educational team comprised of local, state, and national interests. The federal government was buying into the partnership. Fourth, the federal board as the overseer of the programs in all the states could bring about a nationwide standardization in vocational education.[54]

Recognition of Commercial Education

The Smith-Hughes Act contained no provisions for the use of federal funds for vocational courses in commercial education. Education for careers in commerce and business was widespread with many thousands of students enrolled in such courses. However, the area of commercial education was not included when the Smith-Hughes Act was drafted nor was it included during the congressional debating and amending process. There is some indication that the exclusion of commercial education was a deliberate and calculated move by the proponents of Smith-Hughes. William T. Bawden, a leader in commercial education and a staff member of the United States Office of Education, believed that the backers of Smith-Hughes dropped commercial education because they feared the wrath of the private business colleges. Supposedly these people felt that the private business colleges, which were geographically widespread and well respected, could influence enough votes to defeat the bill if commercial education was a part of it. The proponents of Smith-Hughes believed that including commerical education in the bill would be a direct challenge to these business colleges. Bawden found the attitude among the vocation leaders to be one of wait until the time is right and then get federal funds for commercial education. In their opinion, the time was not right in 1917.[55]

Creation of Commercial Education Posts by the Federal Board

Whereas Smith-Hughes did not allocate funds for commercial education, it did authorize the Federal Board for Vocational Education to provide advice and guidance for such programs. Section 6, paragraph 2 of the act stated:

> The board shall have power to co-operate with state boards in carrying out the provisions of this Act. It shall be the duty of the Federal Board for Vocational Education to make, or cause to have made studies, investigations, and reports with particular reference to their use in aiding the states in the establishment of vocational schools and classes and in giving instruction in agriculture, trades and industries, commerce and commercial pursuits, and home economics. Such studies, investigations and reports shall include agriculture and agricultural processes and requirements upon agricultural workers; trades, industries, and apprenticeships, trade and industrial requirements upon industrial workers, and classification of industrial processes and pursuits; commerce and commercial pursuits and requirements upon commercial workers; home management, domestic science, and the study of related facts and principles; and problems of administration of vocational schools and of courses of study and instruction in vocational subjects.[56]

Based upon this authorization, the board included commercial education in its organizational structure almost from its beginning. In 1917, it created a division of Commercial Education and appointed Dr. Cheesman A. Herrick as a special agent for Commercial Education. Herrick, however, could only serve on a part-time basis. In March 1918, the federal board appointed Frederick G. Nichols to be the assistant director for Commercial Education. Nichols—whose activities were noted in Chapter 1—served in this post until early 1921. Although commercial education included the traditional skills such as bookkeeping, typing, and shorthand, the appointment of Nichols as the assistant director was an indication of the interest of the federal board in cooperative retail selling training programs—distributive education. This interest was accentuated in 1919 with the appointment of Isabel C. Bacon as special agent for Retail Selling. Ms. Bacon was a protégé of Lucinda Prince and served as the director of the cooperative retail selling program in the Boston school system.[57]

Decisions on Retail Selling

Directors Prosser and Nichols actively promoted commercial education and, in particular, cooperative retail selling. The year 1919 was a significant one for federal activity in store training. The Federal Board, guided by Nichols and Prosser, issued a lengthy and important bulletin on retail selling and it ruled on the use of federal funds for certain vocational programs in commercial education. The publication was Bulletin No. 22, Series No. 1 titled *Retail Selling Education* written by Lucinda Prince and Isabel Bacon. The bulletin became a basic reference in the field of retail training. The bulletin contained 103 pages and the initial run of fifteen thousand copies was exhausted within six months. At that time, the bulletin was revised and an additional ten thousand copies were printed. This supply also was soon depleted. The speed at which these twenty-five thousand copies were requested and distributed is another indication of the growing interest concerning the training for store employment.[58]

Through the efforts of Nichols and Prosser, the Federal Board agreed in 1919 that certain commercial education programs which existed under specific conditions were eligible for federal funds. The board ruled that federal funds could be used to reimburse the states for the costs of conducting two types of commercial education classes provided they were included in the states' plan for vocational education: First, classes held in evening schools for those office or store workers wishing to improve their skills or for those who desire to prepare for specific office or store jobs. Second, special classes structured on a cooperative plan for students over fourteen years of age who are regularly employed in stores and offices who are also regularly enrolled in school. According to Nichols, the board agreed such classes were part-time programs and part-time programs—including cooperative training could be funded under the act because they were designed to improve the worker's civic and vocational knowledge. However, the funds allocated under Smith-Hughes were all earmarked for specific types of vocational education. The ruling by the board that commercial education was eligible for funding rested on the interpretation by the board that commercial education could, in some ways, be considered as an extension of other types of vocational education—particularly industrial education. However, the other programs, especially industrial education, did not have any extensive surpluses of funds. Therefore, even with the ruling there was no nationwide attempt to fund commercial education. Funding was sporadic and occurred only where local administrators felt they could justify the diversion of funds. Those commercial programs that were funded, including retail selling, received mostly industrial money. All of the efforts of the board, Prosser, and Nichols notwithstanding, commercial education and retail selling were the stepchildren of the Smith-Hughes Act. They were recognized as existing but received only the leftovers. Their future still lay ahead of them.[59]

3 Coming of Age: Vocational Education in the 1920s and 1930s

Vocational Education with Federal Assistance: 1918–1936

Development of the Programs in the States

State Boards. The Smith-Hughes Act required that each state, as a prerequisite to receiving federal funds, meet certain criteria. One of these was the establishment of a state board to oversee vocational education within that state. The legislature of each state was to establish a board of not less than three members that would represent the various interests concerned with vocational education. Most of the states created state boards of vocational education that were separate from other existing agencies. However, some states provided that the State Board of Education or the State Board of Regents would also constitute the State Board of Vocational Education.[1]

Submission of State Plans. Each participating state was required under the Smith-Hughes Act to develop and file with the federal board a plan for vocational education. This plan was to set the guidelines for the state concerning the vocational programs it developed and the goals it wished to achieve. Under the procedure that developed, a state drew up its plan, submitted it to the federal board, revised it until it was acceptable to both parties, and then the state was eligible to receive federal funds. The Federal Board established guidelines for the states to follow in developing their plans. The guidelines called for the state plans to cover the eight basic topics as stated in the Smith-Hughes Act: (1) the type of vocational education that would be provided, (2) the type of schools to be established and equipment to be used, (3) the courses to be taught in each program, (4) the instructional methods to be used, (5) the qualifications of instructors, (6) the qualifications of agriculture directors and supervisions, (7) the

71

training of instructors, and (8) the methods of supervision for agricultural education.[2]

Initially, the states were to submit their plans annually. This placed a great burden on both the states and the federal board. In 1922, the Federal Board proposed that the states draw up a plan which would span a five-year period. Thereafter, the states drew up plans outlining their goals and proposed activities for the next five years. The states, however, could submit revisions for these plans if the need arose during the five years covered by the plans.[3]

General Features of the Developed Programs

Expenditures. The funds allocated under the Smith-Hughes Act were earmarked by the act for specific purposes. Funds were designated for agricultural, industrial, and home economics programs. By 1926, the Smith-Hughes Act was providing an annual allotment in excess of $7 million. The stated purpose of the Smith-Hughes Act was to stimulate the development of vocational education through the introduction of federal funds. By 1926 this goal was a success. In that year, the $7 million provided by the federal government represented approximately one-third of all vocational education financing. The trend for the federal role in the total funding of vocational education has been one of decrease. The federal appropriations continued but the participation of the states and local agencies increased more rapidly than federal funds. The noticeable exception to this trend came during the Great Depression when decreasing income forced the states and the local agencies to cut back their share of the funding. Even during one of the worst of these years, 1935, the states and local authorities provided well over one-half of the total funding.[4]

The funding of vocational education under Smith-Hughes was not without its critics. One criticism leveled at the financing of vocational education challenged the success of the Smith-Hughes Act. Its proponents stated that the concept behind the act was to stimulate the states into developing vocational education. While admitting that the act did stimulate the development of vocational education, they charged that through the 1920s a number of states had violated the spirit of the act by passing the greater share of the nonfederal responsibility to the local school districts. During the 1926–1927 school year, seventeen states provided less than 15 percent of the total funds spent on vocational education within their borders. The local districts in these seventeen states provided from 41 to 76 percent of all the funds. The critics charged these states were not complying with the spirit of the law.[5]

Enrollment. During the first year after the passage of the Smith-Hughes Act, programs enrolling approximately 165,000 students were approved and funded in accordance with the act. As more programs were approved, the enrollment under Smith-Hughes grew to more than 1,249,000 in 1935. Enrollment increased steadily through most of this period. A slight setback in the growth of enrollment occurred during the depths of the Great Depression—1932–1934, primarily as a result of the decline of enrollment in trades and industry programs. Between 1930 and 1934, enrollment in these programs dropped approximately 25 percent. In the same period, the enrollment in agriculture and home economics increased—but not enough to offset the decline in trades and industry. By 1935, enrollment in trades and industry had recovered and the total enrollment figures had exceeded those of 1932.[6]

When vocational enrollment is examined according to the type of school—full-time, part-time, and evening—a similar pattern appears. Enrollment in part-time programs declined after 1928 and did not begin to increase until 1935. Evening programs showed an enrollment decrease after 1932 and did not recover until 1938. Enrollment in full-time programs, however, climbed steadily throughout the 1917–1936 time period. In fact, between 1931 and 1933, enrollment in full-time programs went from the lowest of the three programs to the highest.[7]

Types of Vocational Programs. The Smith-Hughes Act recognized and funded three basic vocational fields—agriculture, trade and industry, and home economics. It also gave similar recognition and funding to three types of schools—full-time, part-time, and evening. Since the purpose of the act was to stimulate vocational education and not to exercise complete control over it, there was little uniformity in programs. The state plans for vocational education that the Federal Board approved were drawn up by each state according to its needs. Heavily industrialized states usually placed greater emphasis on industrial programs whereas states with a greater amount of rural population usually viewed agricultural training as the most important. However, needs were different even within a state. As a result, courses in any of the major fields were taught in different types of schools with different emphasis and for different purposes. The hope was that by filling that local needs the national needs would also be filled.[8]

Almost from the time of its inception, the Federal Board for

Vocational Education was involved in projects that went beyond the preparation of the average citizen for employment in agriculture, industry, or domestic science. Between 1917 and 1936, the Federal Board was also involved in special projects that concerned the training of civilian and military personnel during World War I, rehabilitation of disabled civilians and veterans, and several relief projects during the Depression.

In August 1917 the federal board determined that it could undertake research projects designed to assist the states in planning for the civilian and military needs of the war effort. The board believed that such studies were legitimate activities under the Smith-Hughes Act. As a result of these studies, the federal board assisted in the planning, administration, and coordination of war-related training programs. It assisted in the training of civilian and military personnel in shipbuilding occupations, welding, auto mechanics, management training, radio operators, machinists, and numerous others. In this manner, the federal board and vocational education in general was extremely important to the American war effort.[9]

Early in 1918 the Federal Board for Vocational Education was requested by a Senate resolution to provide information concerning the vocational rehabilitation of military personnel. The board had a prior interest in rehabilitation and at the time of the resolution it had the needed information on hand in the form of a research report. As a result, a bill was introduced in April by Senator Hoke Smith of Georgia—a sponsor of the Smith-Hughes Act—and Representative William J. Sears of Florida that called for the vocational rehabilitation of military personnel disabled in the war effort. The proposal originally contained a provision that also covered disabled civilians. This section was dropped from the bill with the understanding that rehabilitation of civilians would be considered at a later date. The Smith-Sears bill was signed into law by President Woodrow Wilson in June 1918. The federal board immediately began the task of supervising the vocational rehabilitation of disabled soldiers and sailors.[10].

Shortly after the passage of the Smith-Sears Act, Senator Smith introduced a bill into the Senate that called for the vocational rehabilitation of civilians disabled in industry or other occupations. Representative William Bankhead of Alabama introduced a similar bill into the House. Both bills received favorable reports in committee but the Congress did not act upon them. Later, Senator Smith and Representative Simeon Fess of Ohio introduced a bill similar to the Smith-Bankhead Bill. This bill, known as the Smith-Fess Bill, was passed and signed into law in June 1920. Like its predecessor, it provided for the vocational rehabilitation of disabled civilians. This act provided funds for a period of four years. However, the Congress passed supplemental legislation in 1924, 1930, and 1932 to continue the rehabilitation programs established by Smith-Fess.[11]

The Federal Board for Vocational Education also became involved with a number of New Deal agencies in relief projects. Chief among these were the Works Progress Administration (W P A), the Civilian Conservation Corps (C C C), and the National Youth Administration (N Y A). Early in 1933, the federal board and a number of state boards volunteered to assist the relief agencies. As a result, the federal board and the state organizations aided in the preparation of programs, the development of course materials, the acquisition of qualified teachers, and the training of agency supervisors. The vocational education people were deeply involved in the preparation of courses for the C C C. Among the subjects taught in C C C camps that were heavily influenced by vocational education were auto mechanics, soil conservation, drafting, surveying, carpentry, masonry, cooking (to train cooks for the camps), and radio repair. Although federal funds allotted under Smith-Hughes could not be used to pay teachers and buy supplies, the federal board did justify its planning and advisory activities as being within the scope of the functions allowed by the act. Thus it ensured the most effective use of other federal funds and encouraged the participation of the states.[12]

Programs for Black Americans. The funds appropriated under the Smith-Hughes Act were restricted for programs in less than college-level courses. The funds were distributed on the basis of the population of a state and its proportion of the national population. Unlike some of its predecessors, the Smith-Hughes Act did not contain provisions protecting the interests of racial minorities. The individual states drew up their plans for vocational education and the extent that programs for blacks were included was a matter left to the discretion of each state. As a result, programs for blacks did not receive the same level of funding as did programs for whites. This was particularly true in the southern states that contained the greatest percentage of the black population. Rarely were vocational programs for blacks funded in accordance with their percentage of the population of a state. A disproportionate amount of the funds from Smith-Hughes went to support vocational education opportunities for white Americans.[13]

Teacher Training. The Smith-Hughes Act provided an annual appropriation exceeding $1 million for the specific purpose of training vocational teachers. The act required that each federal dollar spent by the state in teacher training be matched by at least $1 from the state or local district. It also required that not more than 60 percent or less than 20 percent of a state's allotted funds could be spent in the training of each of the three main types of vocational teachers recognized by the Act—agriculture (teachers, directors, and supervisors), trades and industry, and home economics. A provision was also included that made a state ineligible for federal reimbursement funds for the salaries of teachers, directors, and supervisors until it had met the minimum 20 percent expenditure for teachers in each of major categories.[14]

Whereas the states offered several procedures to obtain and train qualified vocational teachers, by the mid-1930s a certain degree of informed standardization had been achieved. By that time, the minimum requirement for a teacher of vocational agriculture or home economics was a bachelor's degree from a college designated as a teacher-training institution by the state board for vocational education. In these fields, the actual work experience became secondary to the scientific knowledge gained through education. The work experience was gained either as a part of the curriculum or through a program of summer employment.[15]

The training of vocational teachers in the area of trade and industry took different forms depending upon the particular subject. In some areas, such as the basic skills in wood and metalworking, the basic requirement for teachers became a bachelor's degree in the related areas. In other areas that required years to master the skills involved, highly skilled craftsmen with an aptitude for teaching were training in the basic teaching skills and employed as vocational teachers. These people not only knew their particular skills but were also familiar with the working conditions and methods of the job.[6]

One vocational area was not specifically mentioned in the Smith-Hughes Act nor was it listed by name in the section of the act pertaining to teacher training. This was retail selling or distributive education. As discussed in the previous chapters, interest in retail selling was growing by 1917. The need for qualified teachers of retail selling was growing at a faster rate than could be met by the teacher-training institutions. In the years preeceding the Smith-Hughes Act, the Prince School, founded and administered by Lucinda Prince, was the primary source for teachers of retail selling. Other institutions were becoming involved in the training of retail selling teachers. By 1919 Carnegie Institute of Technology, New York University, Washington University, and State University of Iowa were offering courses in retail selling in either regular or summer sessions. The Federal Board for Vocational Education also became involved in the training of retail selling teachers. In 1919 the board employed a special agent for retail selling who spent a large portion of her time working with the states on the formation of teacher-training programs, the development of courses, and other matters related to the training of retail selling teachers.[17]

Retail Selling with Federal Assistance: 1918–1936

Efforts in Washington. The federal board did not limit itself to assisting in the development of teacher-training programs in retail selling. In 1919, it published the famous Bulletin Number 22 entitled *Retail Selling* by Lucinda Prince and Isabel Bacon. This bulletin, discussed in the preceding chapter, was extremely popular and went through several printings. It served as the basis for numerous training programs in retail selling. The federal board and its special agent for retail selling made a continuous effort to get many business education people to recognize retail selling as a business endeavor. However, there was an ingrained prejudice among many in business education that considered selling to be a second-class occupation. The federal board never gave up. It always insisted that retail selling was a legitimate business endeavor.[18].

Because the Smith-Hughes Act did not make specific provisions for aid to retail selling, the federal board was limited in the monetary stimulus that it could provide for programs in selling. A ruling of the federal board in 1918 made it possible to fund part-time programs in retail selling if funds could be obtained from one of the specified allocations under the Smith-Hughes Act. This ruling was made under that section of the act which authorized training that would improve the civic and vocational ability of workers. The implementation of the ruling also took the view that cooperative training—the essence of retailing selling programs— was in fact a part-time program. When funds could be obtained, the federal board approved vocational programs in retail selling. However, the funds were scarce and the programs were therefore few. Most of the programs that were offered were not organized by business education people but by those in other fields. In fact, most of the impetus and the funds for this program came from the trade and industry people.[19].

Types and Extent of Programs Developed. During the years between the passage of the Smith-Hughes Act and the enactment of the George-Deen Bill, the retail selling programs that were developed under the guidance of federal and state officials were of two types—extension and cooperative. Because of the funding problem and the prejudice of those in business education, most of the early efforts went into extension programs for those already employed in retail selling. Generally these programs consisted of several short courses concerning various aspects of retail selling. These courses were of a few weeks' duration and met after working hours. The employee could take all of the classes or select those that he or she felt would help him the most. Few of these programs were associated with the business education departments in the school systems. Most of these courses were organized, administered, and funded by those in the departments of trade and industry. This was a result of the prevailing attitude of business educators and the fact that most available funding came from that designated for industrial training.[20]

Cooperative training programs in retail selling did exist during this period. However, the nature and structure of these programs seem to have depended on the needs of the community they served and the understanding of those who administered the programs. Some were independent fields of study with well-organized classroom and store training; others were subservient to the commercial education programs in the high schools. In these cases the retail selling students were required to enroll in all or portions of the commercial education programs as well as those special classes in retail selling. Nevertheless, it was estimated that in 1933 about nine thousand five hundred students in forty-nine cities were enrolled in vocational programs that provided some type of cooperative training in retail selling.[21]

Whereas the Smith-Hughes Act established the age of fourteen as the minimum for participation in federally supported programs, most cooperative retail selling programs established sixteen as the minimum age for enrollment. And it gradually developed so that the programs would occupy the students' last two years of high school. There were several reasons why this age and the two-year program were accepted. A major complaint of the participating stores was that a number of the students were immature—too youthful to properly handle the job. Although some fourteen-year-olds could adequately function in the stores, it was generally believed that admitting them would increase rather than improve the problem. Also, through Bulletin No. 22 the federal board had from the beginning envisioned cooperative retail selling as a two-year vocational program. Thus the admission of fourteen-year-olds to the program would find them completing it two years before most store owners would consider them old enough for a fulltime selling position. The federal board believed that it was unfair to train these students for employment when they would not be hired because of their age. Also, those few programs that were of four years' duration and the admitted fourteen-year-olds found a reluctance on the part of the store owners to tolerate a part-time employee for four years. As a result, the concept of a two-year program during the eleventh and twelfth grades for those sixteen years and older was generally accepted by the mid-1930s.[22]

Some of the programs developed between 1917 and 1936 were quite innovative in their scope and methodology. To give the students a feel for store work, several programs included the establishment of model stores. Students in the retail selling program in Omaha, Nebraska, established such a store in 1920. A few years later, the retail selling program at Omaha had two model stores, one of which actually sold a limited variety of items such as novelties and dry goods. These model stores were used to acquaint beginning students with store procedures. The model store is still an integral part of a number of current retail selling programs.[23]

Legislative Changes between Smith-Hughes and George-Deen

Changes in the Federal Board

From July 1917 until October 1933, the Federal Board for Vocational Education existed as an independent agency of the federal government. It was responsible for the administration of the Smith-Hughes Act, the coordination of vocational programs, the supervision of federal vocational funds, and research concerning vocational education. It was as free from improper political interference as other independent agencies, and it won acclaim from Congress on several occasions for its performance and its objectiveness. The board was not, however, without its critics. Those who feared that vocational education would escape from the control of the general education systems had continually agitated against the board and its policies. However, it was not these critics that caused the change in the board's stature. The board fell victim to the same malady that struck down other agencies, businesses, and individuals—the Great Depression. With the decline in personal and governmental income, an economy in government movement began. One way of economizing was to abolish agencies and transfer their responsibilities to the remaining parts of government.[24]

In December 1932, President Herbert Hoover issued an executive order that would abolish the Federal Board for Vocational Education and transfer its functions to the Department of Interior. The board would remain as an advisory body with little or none of its previous authority. Congress, however, blocked the order. When Franklin Roosevelt became president, he also issued an executive order that abolished the board and transferred its functions to the Department of Interior. The board was to be reconstituted as an unpaid advisory body. This order became effective on October 10, 1933, and the Federal Board for Vocational Education ceased to be the chief administrator of federal vocational policy. The new Federal Advisory Board for Vocational Education met infrequently and had little influence on vocational education. It was finally abolished in 1946 under the governmental reorganization plan of President Harry Truman.[25]

Between the enactment of the Smith-Hughes Act and the passage of the George-Deen Bill, several attempts were made in Congress to alter the Smith-Hughes legislation. These attempts ranged from those designed to extend or strengthen Smith-Hughes, to those whose intention was to destroy the legislation of 1917. Of the various efforts to change Smith-Hughes, only two of any importance were successful. These were the George-Reed Act and the George-Ellzey Act.

George-Reed Act

In December 1927, Senator Walter George of Georgia introduced into the Senate a bill to extend additional federal aid to agricultural education and home economics. The following March, Representative Daniel Reed of New York introduced a similar bill into the House. After a year of hearings and debate, the bill was approved by Congress and signed into law by President Calvin Coolidge in February 1929.[26]

The legislation called for an additional appropriation each year for five years to be used for agricultural education and vocational home economics education. The appropriation for the first year would be $500,000 and would increase by $500,000 in each successive year until the amount for the fifth and final year would be $2 million. These funds were to be divided equally between agricultural education and home economics education. The allocation of the agricultural funds to the states and territories was to be on the basis of farm population rather than rural population as the Smith-Hughes Act required. The funds for home economics were to be allocated on the basis of the rural population in the states and territories rather than urban population. Unlike the Smith-Hughes Act, the George-Reed legislation did not make the appropriations an automatic yearly occurrence. It only authorized the appropriation provided that the proposed yearly amounts could be found in the budget. The George-Reed Act differed in another important aspect from the Smith-Hughes Act. Whereas the Smith-Hughes legislation perpetually appropriated certain funds each year, the George-Reed legislation authorized yearly allocations not to exceed those of 1934. Smith-Hughes was to be continual support for vocational education; George-Reed was to be a limited increase—a shot in the arm.[27]

George-Ellzey Act

Concern for vocational education mounted among its proponents as the expiration date of the George-Reed Act approached. Several attempts were made in the early 1930s to extend additional aid to vocational education beyond the expiration date of George-Reed. For various reasons, these attempts failed. However, in early 1934, Senator George and Representative Russell Ellzey of Mississippi introduced similar bills into Congress. These called for an increase in the federal aid given to vocational education and an extension of this aid beyond the 1934 deadline of the George-Reed Act. After considerable debate, the bill was approved by Congress and signed into law by President Franklin Roosevelt in May 1934.[28]

The George-Ellzey Act authorized annual appropriations of $3 million dollars for 1935, 1936, and 1937. These funds were to be divided equally between vocational education in agriculture, trade and industry, and home economics. The money was to be distributed to the states on the basis of their farm population for agricultural education, on the basis of their rural population for home economics education, and on the basis of nonfarm population for education in trade and industries. The act provided that no state would receive less than $5,000 a year for each of the three major types of vocational education. With a few exceptions, the George-Ellzey Act stipulated that the distribution and use of its funds were subject to the same rules and regulations as placed on the funds appropriated under the Smith-Hughes Act.[29]

The George-Deen Act

Senator Walter F. George: Biography

Georgians have had a significant role in shaping the federal legislation for vocational education. Three men from Georgia—Hoke Smith, Dudley Hughes, and Walter F. George—believed that vocational education was vital to the national interest. They championed vocational education by working to improve it and by protecting it from those who would curtail its growth. The efforts of Senator Walter George on behalf of vocational education extended over three decades and included four important pieces of legislation. By profession, Walter George was a lawyer. However, he had strong ties to agriculture as his father was a tenant farmer and young Walter grew up in an agricultural environment. He attended Mercer University in Macon, Georgia, and graduated with a bachelor of science degree in 1900 and received his law degree from that institution in 1901. He successfully practiced law and politics. By 1912 he was a judge of the district court and in 1917 became a justice of the state Supreme Court. George was elected to the United States Senate in 1922 where he served until 1957. In the Senate, George gained a reputation as a conservative and an advocate of states rights. This philosophy, however, did not prohibit his support for vocational education and the use of federal aids for vocational purposes. Hardly a year after the George-Ellzey Act became law, George was again proposing legislation to aid vocational education. This time his efforts were teamed with another Georgian, Representative Braswell D. Deen.[30]

Passage of the George-Deen Act

Like the Smith-Hughes Act, the drafting of the George-Deen Bill was not the work of the men whose names it carried. The movement for the bill was initiated by an agricultural education meeting in Atlanta during the first part of 1935. This group sent a delegation to the commissioner of education with a request for more funds for vocational education. The commission called a conference on the matter that resulted in a resolution concerning vocational education on a national scale. The commission turned the resolution over to the committee on legislation of the American Vocational Association. In early May 1935, this committee drafted a legislative proposal that was given to the champion of vocational education in the Senate—Walter George—who introduced it into the Senate in late May 1935. Companion bills were introduced into the House by several representatives. None of these proposals was reported out of committee during the first session of the Seventy-Fourth Congress. In the second session, Braswell Deen introduced his version of the bill into the House. The Deen Bill differed only slightly from the George Bill.[31]

The George Bill passed the Senate in late April, 1936. The Senate gave it only a minimum of debate. In fact, no hearings were held on the bill and it was given a favorable report by its committee. The House debated the Deen Bill in May. Upon the urging of Representative Deen and others, the House struck all of the Deen Bill after the enacting clause and substituted for it the George Bill that had passed the Senate. The Senate accepted this and the bill was signed into law by President Roosevelt on June 8, 1936. Numerous organizations had supported the George-Deen Act, including the National Grange, the Farm Bureau, and several municipal organizations.[32]

Although the George-Deen Bill was approved by Congress with a certain amount of ease, it was opposed in both houses of Congress. The opposition, however, recognized the merits of vocational education and the need to develop more vocational programs. The major concerns of the opponents were the amounts to be appropriated and the inclusion of vocational fields other than agriculture, trade and industry, and home economics. Some opponents believed that the suggested annual appropriation of $14 million was too much of an increase. These people intended to favor annual appropriations of $6 million. Several members of Congress expressed concern about the inclusion of distributive education in the act. Some readily admitted that they did not know what it was, whereas others vehemently attacked distributive education and any appropriation for support of it. One congressman stated that funds for distributive education would be spent teaching people how to sell gasoline at filling stations. He thought that this was a waste of money and time, and he vigorously urged that distributive education be dropped from the bill. In both cases, the opposition lost. Distributive education and the large increase in funds remained in the bill and was enacted into law.[33]

Provisions of the George-Deen Act

The George-Deen Act authorized annual appropriations for vocational education in the amount of $14,483,000. With the permanent annual appropriation of $7,302,000 under the Smith-Hughes Act, the total amount of federal funds allocated for vocational education could be in excess of $21 million a year. There was, however, one qualification. Whereas the Smith-Hughes Act established a permanent and automatic appropriation, the George-Deen Act only authorized the yearly allocation of funds up to the stated amount. Each year Congress was to determine and approve the amount to be allocated under George-Deen. And it soon became evident that there were those in Congress who were determined to keep the George-Deen appropriation below the authorized amount. During the spring of 1937, a move was launched in Congress and the executive branch to restrict the funds to $6 million or less. The full authorized amount was only approved after much debate and considerable pressure from vocational, agricultural, and business groups.[34]

Under the George-Deen Act, $12 million of the annual appropriations was to be divided equally between agriculture, trade and industry, and home economics. An additional $1 million per year was to be used to train vocational teachers. And, another $1.2 million was designated for the purpose of teaching distributive education. This was the first time that the distributive occupations were specifically covered by a vocational act and the first time that funds were earmarked for their use.[35]

In the George-Deen Act, Congress recognized the conditions of the national economy of 1936, and the critical need of education for funds. The act provided that during the first five years— 1937 to 1942—the state and local authorities would be required to match only 50 percent of the funds provided under George-Deen. After 1942 the percentage required in matching funds would increased by 10 percent a year until all the federal funds were matched by 1947. This provided the immediate boost to vocational education and allowed the states time to develop the economic basis to match the funds.[36]

Inclusion of Distributive Education in the George-Deen Act

Whereas the George-Deen Act specifically included distributive occupations in the list of those vocational areas to receive federal funds, it did not define the term. In February 1937 the Office of Education attempted to state what were distributive occupations and what were not. In its revised policy bulletin, the Office of Education defined distributive occupations as:

> ... those followed by workers directly engaged in merchandising activities, or in direct contact with buyers and sellers when—
> 1. Distributing to consumers, retailers, jobbers, wholesalers, and others, the products of farm and industry;
> 2. Managing, operating, or conducting a commercial service or personal service business, or selling the services of such a business.[37]

The Office of Education continued in its statement with a definition of what was not a distributive occupation.

> Distributive occupations do not include clerical occupations such as stenography, bookkeeping, office clerical work, and the like; nor do they include trade and industrial work followed by those engaged in rail-road, trucking, or other transportation activities.[38]

The major factor in establishing whether or not an occupation was distributive was its relationship to the consumer. If the job called for contact with the consumer or a like agent through buying, selling, managing, or service, then there was little doubt that it was a distributive occupation.

The act did, however, place limitations upon the types of programs that could receive federal funds. Section 6 of the act placed funds appropriated under the authorization of the George-Deen Act under the same rules and restrictions established by the Smith-Hughes Act. Also, Section 6 specifically limited the use of funds for distributive education to part-time and evening schools. Therefore, to be eligible for federal funding, distributive education in a part-time school must be for those of fourteen years or older who are gainfully employed in a distributive occupation. The evening school was limited to those sixteen years or older who were employed in a distributive occupation.[39]

Whereas the George-Deen Act did not specifically cover cooperative training programs in retailing selling, such programs were approved and funded under the ruling issued in 1918 by the

Federal Board for Vocational Education. As previously stated, this ruling held that cooperative programs in which the student spent 50 percent of his school hours employed in a suitable job were part-time programs and eligible for federal funds. Thus, three types of programs in distributive education were eligible for federal aid—part-time, evening, and cooperative part-time. However, during its first years under the George-Deen Act, the cooperative part-time programs made up only a small part of the total number of persons enrolled in distributive education. In 1938, 36,008 persons were enrolled in federally funded vocational distributive education programs. Only 3,600 of these were in cooperative part-time programs. Although the total enrollment in vocational distributive education grew during the following five years, the proportion of these enrolled in cooperative part-time programs declined to about 6 percent.[40]

Criticism of the George-Deen Act

The members of Congress who—as has been noted—attacked the bill during its enactment were not the only critics of the George-Deen Act. Some of those in general education were also critical of the act. An editorial in the March 1937 issue of *The Elementary School Journal* charged that the distribution of funds under the act was unfair. The writer of the editorial maintained that the funds should go where they were most needed. He felt they should be distributed on the basis of the proportion of the national total of school-age children a state contained rather than its proportion of farm population, or rural population, or non-rural population. The editorial continued by charging that it was possible that the act and the federal government were training young people for jobs that were steadily decreasing in number. These complaints notwithstanding, the funds flowed from the George-Deen Act and vocational education—particularly distributive education—prospered.[51]

4 The War Years and After

Developments to the End of World War II

General Vocational Education

Advisory Committee on Education. Although he was an advocate of vocational education, President Franklin Roosevelt was not convinced that the large appropriation authorized by the George-Deen Act was advisable or needed. At the time that he signed the George-Deen Act into law, Roosevelt sent identical letters to Senator George, Representative Deen, and others stating his intention to create a commission to study the area of federal aid to vocational education. On September 19, 1936, Roosevelt formed the President's Committee on Vocational Education, which consisted of eighteen members who were deemed to be impartial in their attitudes toward vocational education. The committee was assigned the duty of evaluating the existing federal aid for vocational education program, of studying the relationship between vocational education and general education and between vocational education and current economic and social conditions, and of determining the need for any additional federal aid to vocational education. The following spring, however, a number of bills were introduced into Congress that called for federal aid not only to vocational education but to general education as well. Because of this, on April 19, 1937, Roosevelt changed the name of the committee, added four more members to it, and expanded its scope of study to include the federal relationship to all education and the conduct of it. The committee became known as the Advisory Committee on Education.[1]

The committee completed its assignment in 1938 and submitted a report containing its recommendations to the president. The committee's report praised parts of the administrative structure of vocational education and called for reform of the other sections. The report recommended the continuation of the minimum age of fourteen for participation in federally funded programs. It praised the restrictions placed upon plant training by the George-Deen Act and recommended that they be extended into other training programs. The committee felt that these restrictions— which required the participating industries to provide training for the students while they worked—protected the student from exploitation by the industries. In the opinion of the committee, there was a need to reform the laws governing the federal aid program. The committee recommended that the states be given more control over the expenditure of federal funds, the organization of the programs, and the administration of vocational education. Also, the committee believed that new legislation was needed to ensure that programs and educational institutions for blacks get their fair share of the federal funds.[2]

The committee and its report were not without their critics. Professor David Snedden of Columbia University, a long-time critic of the type of vocational education that was developing in the United States, found little of value in the report. Snedden charged that the committee did not deal with the problems of vocational education and that the report had a serious case of the disease which he believed infected the current educational philosophies— vagueness and romanticism. He believed that whereas enrollment in vocational programs was high, few of the people who completed these programs were ready to become productive workers. Snedden believed that vocational education offered great promise if it would train the students to what he called "full-competency"—possessing all the skills necessary for immediate productivity in the particular vocation. Snedden charged that neither the federal laws, the state plans for vocational education, nor the Advisory Committee on Education recognized the problem. And none of them offered any hope for remedying the situation.[3]

Vocational Education by War's End. The growth of vocational programs steadily increased from the time of Smith-Hughes to the end of World War II. A general overview of this growth can be obtained by an examination of the activities in trade and industrial education. In the early 1920s, trade and industrial education offered major programs in fifty occupational areas. In 1944 this number had grown to eighty-five—a 70 percent increase in two decades. An effort was made in trade and industrial education to keep pace with changes in technology as a number of the programs added by 1944 were in occupations that did not exist in 1920.[4]

As had happened in 1917, the involvement of the United States in World War II brought new duties, new problems, and new funds to vocational education. The war effort needed trained workers for the defense industries. Vocational programs were established to train workers in the needed skills. Some of these programs were organized as part of the existing vocational education systems, whereas others were established through separate agencies and institutions. Whatever their parentage, these special defense-oriented programs brought additional federal appropriations in excess of $389 million to vocational education between 1940 and 1945, approximately 19 percent of which went to agricultural programs. The remainder was used to train workers in trade and industrial skills for the defense industries. These exclusively defense-related training programs had a total enrollment in excess of 11,500,000 for the period of July 1940 to April 1945.[5]

The war created an abnormal demand for labor. Because of the need for workers, many people joined the work force who otherwise would not have been seeking employment. Some of these, and many of the regular work force, were trained for defense jobs that would cease to exist once the war ended. The leaders in government and in vocational education realized that the period of readjustment which would follow the war would cause serious problems for the nation, the economy, and the workers. Whereas many workers could make the transition from defense industry to peacetime employment, many others would require additional training. Some of these would need only refresher courses or courses designed to increase their knowledge and skills in their job areas. Others would require retraining in completely different fields of employment. The task of training workers for the postwar period was as difficult as training them for emergency defense jobs.[6]

The Attitude of Labor. Organized labor played a significant role in the drive to pass the Smith-Hughes Act of 1917. Labor had overcome its misgivings concerning vocational education and had joined in the effort. However, by the time President Roosevelt created the Advisory Committee on Education, labor believed that its worst fears about vocational education had become reality. A study entitled "The Experience of Labor with Trade and Industrial Education" by Howell H. Broach and Julia O'Connor Parker was completed in 1938 under the auspices of the Advisory Committee. The researchers found that the vast majority of organized labor felt it had been betrayed by vocational educators. Labor believed that public money was being spent for the good of the educators and the private interests—management. As far as labor was concerned, it had been ignored, it advice disregarded, and its interest overshadowed by that of management. The disenchantment of labor was such that in 1937 the American Federation of Labor opposed the appropriations for the George-Deen Act. The research team found, however, that in those states in which labor had been made an active participant in the administration of vocational education, its advice sought, and its interests considered, the attitude of labor toward vocational education was inclined to be favorable. The study noted that much of the abuse suffered by labor was the result of a prevailing, and, in some cases open, hostility among some segments of vocational education toward organized labor. The research team recommended that federal legislation be passed to ensure the participation of labor in the administration of vocational programs. It also recommended that restrictions be placed on certain activities in vocational training in order to protect the interest of organized labor—e.g. the contracting of out-of-school work.[7]

Distributive Education

Pre-War Activities. In 1938, slightly more than 36,000 persons were enrolled in accredited distributive education programs, which operated in 345 cities and towns. By 1944, enrollment in distributive education had grown by 504 percent. In that year, training programs serving 181,500 persons were being conducted in about 1,200 cities and towns. Also during this period, the combined expenditures of federal, state, and local funds had more than doubled. Other trends were also noticeable during this period. Distributive education was extended into the smaller cities, and employees of smaller businesses were taking the training. Also there was a change in the curriculum of the programs. The basic course in general salesmanship was being supplemented by courses in sales and merchandising that were oriented for specific types of commercial enterprises.[8]

Two important conferences concerning distributive education were held between the passage of the George-Deen Act and the end of World War II. The first was held in 1939 at the Dunwoody Institute in Minneapolis. The focus of this conference was on training for adult employees in distributive occupations and the training of experienced workers to be teachers. The second conference took place in 1942 in Washington, D.C. This conference was concerned with the place of distributive education in the war effort. Particular emphasis was placed on the development of programs in the training of supervisory personnel.[9]

Wartime Programs in Distributive Education. Several major programs were developed to meet the wartime needs. Most originated from ideas conceived at the Washington conference. First, a program was established for the rapid training of the new retail employees needed to fill the positions vacated by those entering the armed forces or defense work. Second, a program was developed to instruct experienced store employees on the wartime regulations and how they would affect the buying and selling of goods. Third, a program was designed that would assist store managers, department heads, and supervisors with the development of in-service or on-the-job training sessions within their stores and departments. Fourth, a program was established to provide store owners and managers with instruction concerning the wartime regulations, controls, and laws under which their businesses would operate. These programs were referred to as business clinics rather than management retraining sessions or some other equally applicable term. Probably the term *clinic* was thought to be more appropriate considering the economic and social status of those in attendance. A fifth program also concerning those in management and supervisory positions was also developed. This program dealt with human relations and was designed to improve the effectiveness of the supervisors in dealing with their employees. The object was to improve the quality of the employees' work by showing the manager how to communicate and relate with the employees.[10]

Another impact of the war on distributive education was the decrease in enrollment in the programs offered through the evening extension classes. This was coupled with an increased enrollment in part-time extension classes. Several reasons were noted for the decrease in evening enrollments. For the convenience of defense workers, stores were kept open later in the evenings; store employees were active after store hours in civilian defense programs; and, persons were employed as store workers who were not planning to stay in retail work after the war. Among the reasons cited for the increase in part-time enrollments was the willingness of employers to give employees free time with pay to attend such classes. This was viewed as evidence of the growing appreciation of businessmen for distributive education programs.[11]

Enrollment in cooperative part-time distributive training programs on the secondary school level grew during the war years.

This enrollment grew in spite of the decrease in the number of seniors in the high schools. However, many post-high school and junior college programs were discontinued. Wartime cooperative distributive training became primarily the concern of the high schools.[12]

General Vocational Education in Wartime

Vocational education was gearing up for its part in the national defense programs long before the United States actually became involved in World War II. By mid-1940, a special program known as Vocational Education for National Defense or VEND was in operation. This program, later called Vocational Training for War Production Workers or VTWPW, received massive appropriations throughout the war to train workers in those skills needed in the defense industries. It was this program that received the mass of the aforementioned $389,000,000 and trained over 11,500,000 workers.[13]

The legislation passed in 1940 that established the VEND program provided only $49 million; the rest was appropriated by subsequent legislation from 1940 until the end of the war. The legislation passed in 1940, however, did provide the basic patterns that later acts followed concerning the regulation, distribution, and use of these special appropriations. The VEND funds were to be administered through the Office of Education in a manner similar to that in which the funds supplied by Smith-Hughes and George-Deen were administered. There were, however, some noteworthy differences. First, the regular funds under the Smith-Hughes and George-Deen Acts required matching funds from state or local sources. There were no matching requirements attached to VEND funds. These programs could be entirely federally financed. Second, there were restrictions concerning the use of regular vocational funds to train teachers and to pay portions of their salaries. There were no such restrictions on VEND funds. Third, the selection of students to receive training under the regular vocational program was the responsibility of the individual schools. Federal legislation required that certain programs under VEND be filled from those seeking jobs through the public employment services. Fourth, regular vocational funds were required by law to be distributed to the states on the basis of population. The VEND funds were to be distributed according to the need of the defense industries without consideration of population.[14]

The training provided by the VEND programs provided preemployment training and supplemental training in numerous jobs, and programs in the training of supervisors and foremen were offered. The program also trained about 206,999 military personnel—both men and women—in such jobs as welding, aircraft mechanics, radio, electrical and machine skills, and riveting. Also over 400,000 civilian employees of the military services were trained in similar skills. In one fourteen-month period (May 1942–June 1943), the VEND trained nearly 60,000 people for jobs with the Signal Corps. As the war came to an end, the training programs were halted. The burst of money that came so quickly ended just as suddenly. The Office of Education issued a memorandum on May 5, 1945, ordering the training programs to end. Within a short time, the dismantling of the wartime training programs began.[15]

The Postwar Situation

National Scene: The Full Employment Act of 1946

Jobs in the postwar era was a matter that had concerned a number of individuals, organizations, and government officials. Even before the war ended, these parties were studying the problems of employment in the postwar period. A concept that was popular with this group was what became known as "full employment." Basically, full employment existed when the demand for goods and services was great enough to require the employment of the total available work force in order to meet the demand. In 1944 the popular belief was that the United States would need a total of 60 million jobs in the postwar era. This meant that 60 million jobs would ensure employment for everyone who was able and willing to work. This number also included those in the military and those working for local, state, and federal government. Those closer to the situation and with a greater knowledge of economics projected that full employment could probably be reached with a total of 55 or 56 million jobs. Nevertheless, these lower figures represented a 3 to 4 million increase over the total number of employed civilians in 1944—the height of the wartime employment. The problem, however, was much more than these figures might lead one to believe. With the release of approximately 12 million persons from the armed services and the termination of several million defense jobs, it can be seen why some economists saw the possibility of an unemployment figure for the postwar years numbering nearly 20 million.[16]

The role of the federal government in ensuring an adequate number of jobs for the work force had been a concern of several officials—including President Franklin Roosevelt. On several occasions—particularly during the early 1940s—Roosevelt expressed his belief that some method should be devised that would ensure employment for those in the work force. Roosevelt saw employment as a right. He believed that it was the responsibility of the federal government to protect the right of the individual to have a job and to be productive. Under Roosevelt's leadership, the federal government had gained some experience in the field of providing jobs through the work-relief programs of the New Deal. These jobs, however, were emergency programs and not the full-time economically and socially productive jobs envisioned by Roosevelt and others in the concept of "full employment."[17]

The proposal concerning the method the federal government should use in obtaining full employment developed out of work of the War Contracts subcommittee of the Senate Military Affairs Committee during the last half of 1944. On January 12, 1945, Senator James Murray of Montana introduced a bill into the Senate that was based on the report of the subcommittee. A month later, a similar bill was introduced into the House by Representative Wright Patman of Texas. Simply stated, the bill called for the president to present to Congress each year an estimate of the work force for that year, an estimate of the total amount of investment and expenditures necessary to provide jobs for the work force, and an estimate of all projected expenditures by all private and public entities. If the projected expenditures were less than what was the estimated need, the president was to propose ways in which federal expenditures would be manipulated in order to provide the necessary investments. If possible, the federal government was to use its funds in ways that would encourage the private sector of the economy to produce the needed jobs.[18]

After heated debate in the Senate, the House, and the Conference Committee, a revised bill was approved by both houses in February 1946. President Harry Truman signed it into law on February 20, 1946. Along with the basics from the Murray Bill, the Full Employment Act of 1946 also contained provisions for the establishment of a Council of Economic Advisors. This council would be under the president and its members would be appointed by him with the approval of the Senate. The duties of the Council of Economic Advisors were to assist the president in the preparation of the annual report to the Congress and to keep a continual surveillance on the economic conditions within the nation.[19]

The concern about the postwar economic situation and the problems of providing jobs in the peacetime economy was widespread among both the supporters and the opponents of the Full Employment Act of 1946. The differences arose over the need for, and the degree of, government involvement in peacetime economic conditions. Even among the proponents of the act, the degree of support ran the gamut from total commitment to reluctant approval. Organized labor was a good example of the latter. While supporting the act, labor vigorously urged Congress to include in the act or to enact separately measures to protect the interest of labor through higher minimum wages, fair employment practices, and other labor-oriented legislation.[20]

Postwar Problems in American Education

World War II emphasized problems in American education that were previously recognized by astute observers of the educational system. Data from sources such as the induction centers for the armed services revealed that the level of mental and physical achievement varied greatly over the nation. Numerous persons from certain geographic regions or certain educational environments were rejected for military service because of test scores that reflected inadequate educational preparation. Leaders in the field of education had for years been aware of these varying achievement levels and of the elements in the system that produced them. It was generally conceded that the causes of this variance were the inequalities in such things as the funds expended per student, amount and adequacy of equipment, number of students in attendance, funds available for salaries and supplies, and numerous other items that varied from state to state and school district to school district. The difference between school districts could be staggering. For example, the annual cost per teaching unit that included classroom maintenance, equipment, books, supplies, and salaries varied from under $100 per unit to nearly $6,000 per unit in 1939–40. And in most cases, the areas with the lowest unit cost contained the greatest number of school-age children. Overcrowding and inadequate funding were not conducive to the production of the educational levels deemed necessary for the maintenance of a democratic society.[21]

Another problem facing American education in the postwar period was the diversity of the student body. What homogeneity that had existed in the student body during the prewar period was shattered following the war. School systems were faced with having within the system, and even within the same classrooms, individuals whose education had not been interrupted by the war, those who had dropped out to work in the defense industries, disabled veterans, and returning service personnel. The problems of making the necessary adjustments in order to serve this diverse group fell heavily on the colleges and on the secondary schools. The elementary schools faced another problem that held implications for all levels of education. The first wave of the so-called "war babies" began to enter the educational system in 1946. With this rapid growth in school population, the severity of financial problems facing American education increased.[22]

Faced with these problems of population, equipment, and finance, a number of those in education looked to the federal government for assistance. President Franklin Roosevelt had provided some financial assistance to schools through the emergency programs of the New Deal, and he spoke of the need and the duty of the nation to provide adequate education for all. In his Annual Message to Congress on January 21, 1946, President Harry Truman requested that Congress enacted legislation to "provide financial aid to assist the States in assuring more nearly equal opportunities for a good education." Even Truman's assurance that the federal government would not seek to dominate education did not still the fears of those who feared the loss of state and local control over education.[23]

Postwar Attitudes toward Vocational Education

The attitudes toward vocational education in the postwar period were based upon its performance before and during the war. These attitudes were shaped by a montage of conflicting evaluations of the effectiveness and success of vocational education. The opinion with probably the largest following held that vocational education was an overwhelming success and that it was partly responsible for the allied victory in World War II. Those accepting this view pointed to the massive number of defense workers and military personnel who had been trained for war-related jobs between 1940 and 1945. Vocational education, they said, had won the war because of its ability to provide quality job training. Without vocational education, the war effort would have been greatly hampered.[24]

A second and much smaller group, consisting primarily of those in the traditional forms of education, charged that vocational education was a complete failure. They also pointed to the wartime activities in vocational education for the proof of their charges. Vocational education, they contended, did not train competent workers with vocational skills. Instead, it produced operators who were trained only in one particular skill, workers who understood only their small part of the operation and whose jobs would be rapidly eliminated through changing technology. This group charged that of the massive number of workers trained during the war, the vast majority would require much retraining in order to find and keep a peacetime job. These people, typified by Robert M. Hutchins, the chancellor of the University of Chicago, charged that industry was better able to train workers than was vocational education. They contended that American education should return to a broadly based general education which prepared students for life rather than for making a living. This, it was believed, would produce a better informed and better adjusted citizenry, and it would produce individuals with better basic educational skills.[25]

A third and smaller group took a position between the avid pro and rabid antivocational education forces. This group consisted of vocational educators who were enthusiastic about vocational training but who also accepted as valid some of the criticism leveled at vocational education. These people agreed with the critics that the wartime training did not produce workers with vocational skills. However, they contended that what had occurred during the war was not vocational education per se; it was in fact only emergency wartime training. Therefore, they agreed that massive retraining programs would be needed for many wartime workers during the postwar period. Furthermore, they stressed that in a sound vocational program the students were also well grounded in the elements of a liberal arts education. Thus the true vocational student was prepared for life as well as for making a living.[26]

Whatever their stand concerning the success of the wartime vocational programs, a generally accepted view by all groups was that education—either traditional or vocational—faced difficult problems during the postwar period. It was expected that a massive increase in the number of students would occur in both general and vocational education. The problems of overcrowding, financial deficiencies, mixed student bodies, and retraining concerned all. However, in the area of public opinion, those viewing vocational education as successful and as a major contributor to the winning of the war seemed to have emerged the winner. If in fact Congress reflects the attitudes of the electorate, then the passage of the George-Barden Act of 1946 has been viewed as a reward given to vocational education for its meritorious wartime service.[27]

The Postwar Reward for Vocational Education

The Passage of the George-Barden Act

In May 1944, Senator Walter George of Georgia and six other members of the Senate introduced a bill providing for additional aid to vocational education. No action was taken on the bill during that session so he reintroduced the measure in the next session—February 1945. The following fall, Representative Graham A. Barden of North Carolina introduced a similar but slightly different bill into the House. The Senate passed its revision of the bill and forwarded it to the House. The House amended the Senate bill by substituting parts of its bill. After a conference, both houses passed a revised form of the Senate bill and President Truman signed it into law on August 1, 1946.[28]

The Senate and the House hearings on their respective bills revealed considerable criticism of vocational education and suggestions to remedy the situation. This was particularly true in the cases of business education and distributive education. The private business and technical schools—the old nemesis of public supported vocational education—attacked the George-Barden proposals. During the Senate hearings held in May 1945, Dr. J. S. Noffsinger, representing the National Council of Business Schools, delivered a seething attack upon the George bill and vocational education. Noffsinger charged that the bills were ill conceived, unwarranted, and wasteful. He believed that the bills were an attempt by vocational education interests to grab all the federal funds they could before the government began its postwar economy measures. Noffsinger contended that a number of the proposed programs to be funded were not necessary because in some areas the vocational programs were turning out too many individuals who were not properly prepared. He cited documents from the United States Office of Education that stated that over one-half of those graduating from high school commercial education programs were not qualified to find or hold jobs. Noffsinger also cited a report by the state commissioner of education in Connecticut that estimated that there would need to be an annual turnover of 27 percent of all employed stenographers in the state if those graduating each spring from the high schools as stenographers were to find jobs. Noffsinger's testimony struck hard on the themes of waste and giveaways in the bills and failures within the vocational education programs. His testimony, though primarily aimed at business education, generally supported those in the postwar period who charged that vocational education was not producing adequately trained graduates.[29]

Organized labor opposed the George-Barden proposals. Labor, an early proponent of vocational education, had become disillusioned with vocational training. And in the postwar period, labor continued to believe that management was using vocational education against the interest of labor. In a statement read before the Senate Education and Labor Committee, the American Federation of Labor opposed the George-Barden proposals and urged American education to return to the more broadly based general education. The A F L charged that vocational education was producing poorly trained specialists in narrow fields. It argued that the nation would profit more from students who were educated in the general tradition of liberal arts and then trained for skilled positions through apprenticeships than from those individuals who were trained in the vocational schools and denied a broad-based education. Labor urged that before any additional funds were authorized, the structure of vocational education be altered to reflect this return to the liberal arts.[30]

Among those who testified at the hearings in favor of the bills were several persons who urged Congress to give its approval so that distributive education programs could be continued and improved. These people represented such groups as the National Retail Grocers Association, the Joint National Committee on Distributive Education for Pharmacy, the National Council for Retail Trade Associations, and the publication known as the *American Druggist*. All stressed the need for more training opportunities for store employees through cooperative part-time training in the high schools for the young workers, and part-time and evening programs for the others. John W. McPherrin, the editor of the *American Druggist*, noted that distributive education had only reached less than 2 percent of all of the retail workers in the nation. He also pointed out that the retail group that needed the training the most had participated in distributive education the least. This group included the smaller stores, and particularly the small stores in small towns. McPherrin charged that the distributive education people were partly responsible for this situation. He cited the shortage of funds for new programs in smaller towns and the confusion among those in vocational education concerning how and who should handle distributive programs.[31]

The George-Barden proposals contained other items that also drew heavy criticisms. One of these items was the amount of money the bills proposed to authorize for vocational programs. Under the proposal of Senator Walter George, vocational agriculture would receive an additional annual allotment of $23 million, home economics—$16 million, trades and industries—$16 million, distributive education—$7 million, occupational guidance—$4 million, public service occupations—$2 million, office occupations—$5 million, and supervision of industrial arts education—$5 million. The sums proposed in the Barden bill were slightly smaller. The criticism of these amounts and of the programs to receive them was such that when the final draft of the bill was approved, the provisions for occupational guidance, public service training, office training, and the supervision of industrial arts were dropped. Also the amounts for agriculture, home economics, trades and industries, and distributive education were substantially reduced.[32]

Another item that drew much criticism was the proposal concerning the matching of federal funds by the state and local authorities. The Senate bill provided that no matching funds would be required of the states for two years. By the third year, the states would be required to match 25 percent of the federal funds. The House bill called for the states to match at least 50 percent of the federal expenditures until 1950. From 1950 on the matching requirement would increase by 10 percent a year until the federal funds were being matched 100 percent. This requirement was also greatly changed in the final draft of the bill.[33]

However, the item that received the greatest amount of opposition was the proposal for federal funds to established area vocational schools. The Senate bill provided for an annual appropriation of $24 million for area schools of less than college grade. The House bill proposed an appropriation of $16 million for these schools. Opposition came from not only the private vocational schools but also from those in the traditional sector of education who saw in this proposal an increased threat of a dualistic system of education. This proposal was also dropped from the bill in its final form. It would not, however, be forgotten.[34]

Provisions of the George-Barden Act

Upon receiving final congressional approval and the signature of the president, the Vocational Education Act of 1946—the George-Barden Act—authorized annual appropriations of $10 million for vocational agriculture, $8 million each for home economics and trades and industries, and $2.5 million for distributive education in part-time and evening programs. The act required the states to match any federal funds they received on a dollar-for-dollar basis. It also established a minimum allotment for the states of $40,000 each in agriculture, home economics, and trades and industries. The minimum for distributive education was set at $15,000. Although they were subject to many of the same restrictions established under the Smith-Hughes Act, the funds provided by the George-Barden Act could be used with greater flexibility than funds provided under early acts. There were no requirements concerning the amount of the funds each state was to allot for teacher education, and the funds could be used to acquire equipment. The only provision was that after 1951 only 10 percent of a state's allotment could be used to purchase equipment. In general, the George-Barden Act provided more money for vocational education and a greater flexibility about how it was to be spent.[35]

5 Years of Triumphs and Trials: From the Fair Deal to the New Federalism

The 1950s

DECA

The George-Deen Act of 1936 stimulated an increase in the number of cooperative part-time distributive education programs offered through the secondary schools. As a result, a number of schools during the late 1930s began forming local organizations for the students enrolled in these programs. These groups were known by several names such as "Future Distributors," "Future Retailers," "Future Merchants," "Distributors," and "Distributive Education Clubs." In the early 1940s, several states established statewide organizations for students of distributive education. By 1945 several states were holding state conventions attended by the representatives of the local chapters. These local and state organizations were formed to provide a means of communicating ideas and experiences among the students, to give the students a group identity—a sense of comradeship, and to fill the void in their social lives created when their training forced them to miss regular school functions.[1]

The United States Office of Education in 1946 invited a committee representing the state supervisors of distributive education to meet in Washington, D.C., and develop plans for a national organization for students of distributive education. The first Interstate Conference of Distributive Education Clubs was held at Memphis, Tennessee, in April 1947. There delegates of the twelve states represented at the conference unanimously adopted a resolution calling for the establishment of a national organization. Officers were elected and committees were formed with instructions to prepare a constitution in time for the next annual convention. When the group met in St. Louis in 1948, the convention adopted the proposed constitution and officially named itself The Distributive Education Clubs of America, or in short form DECA. The convention accepted seventeen states as charter members: Georgia, Indiana, Kansas, Kentucky, Louisiana, Michigan, Mississippi, Missouri, North Carolina, Ohio, Oklahoma, South Carolina, Tennessee, Texas, Utah, Virginia, and Washington.[2]

The growth of distributive education and of DECA progressed steadily through the 1950s. When the decade ended, the number of participating states had grown from the original seventeen to thirty-eight. The number of high school distributive education students who were members of DECA grew from nearly eight hundred in 1948 to over nineteen thousand by 1960.[3]

Attacks on Funding for Distributive Education

The late 1940s and the early 1950s were times of mounting interest in governmental economy. Several proposals, some successful, were advanced in this period to cut government spending. One area that was under attack was vocational education in general and distributive education in particular. One proposal that was supported by officials of the National Education Association—the NEA—called for all federal aid for education of all types to be pooled into one fund and the division and administration of these funds be handled through one office. This proposal naturally upset those in vocational education as it would abolish all of the special appropriations that were earmarked by law for their programs. They felt that if these funds were abolished, vocational education would not receive its fair share of public financing. At the 1948 convention of the American Vocational Association (AVA), the executive secretary of the organization —L. H. Dennis—called upon the NEA to define its official position on the proposal to pool funds. The AVA also adopted a resolution that condemned any such plan for pooling federal funds.[4]

The most serious attack on vocational funding originated in the House of Representatives in 1951. In that year, a vocational education appropriations bill was approved by the House and sent to the Senate. The bill contained a clause that prohibited the states from using any of the federal funds for distributive education. This meant that the federal funds for distributive education which were $1,794,499 the preceding year would be cut to zero for

1951–1952. The House Appropriations Committee had approved the bill with the comment that distributive education was not important enough to justify any federal expenditures during a time of economy in governmental spending. The American Vocational Association spearheaded a campaign to delete the crippling clause from the bill. The AVA urged its members and other interested parties to educate their congressmen concerning distributive education and why it was needed. The association called for a massive outpouring of letters and calls to Congress as a means of restoring the funds. The proponents of distributive education rose to the challenge, the letters and calls poured in, and Congress restored slightly over half of the funds—$900,000—for distributive education.[5]

The victory of vocational education in achieving the partial restoration of the distributive education funds did not stop the congressional economy axe from a second swing at distributive education. The following year, Congress again chopped the appropriations for distributive education. And, again the cut was one-half of the previous appropriations—$450,000. In two years the funds for distributive education had been cut by 75 percent. This resulted in a drastic reduction in the number and size of programs and a sharp decline in enrollment. The enrollment figures for 1953 were nearly half of those of 1950. Not until fiscal 1956 would federal spending for distributive education approach the 1951 level. Congress added insult to injury in that during this period—1949–1953—distributive education absorbed the entire amounts cut from all vocational education appropriations. None of the other areas—agriculture, home economics, and trade and industry—was reduced below its 1949 funding level.[6]

Early in 1953 the cause of distribution education received aid from a group with some influence among the members of Congress. The National Retail Dry Goods Association (NRDGA), which represented nearly seven thousand five hundred stores, spoke out in defense of distributive education. Its president, Wade G. McCargo, wrote a letter to the Federal Security Administration, which housed the United States Office of Education. This letter was highly publicized and was published in its entirety with editorial comments in the *Journal of Business Education*, April 1953. McCargo charged that it was unfair for distributive education to bear all the cuts in vocational education funds. He cited the disruption that these cuts caused in the programs. McCargo told of the importance of the distributive education programs and of the value the members of his organization saw in it. He ended his letter with a call not for more funds for vocational education but for a more equitable division of funds between the vocational fields. McCargo's letter and the pressure from the NRDGA have been credited as the reason that the proposed fiscal 1954 budget included a 25 percent across-the-board reduction in federal aid to vocational education with the exception of distributive education. The proposed budget requested that appropriations for distributive education be raised from $450,000 to $1,279,646—a 184.3 percent increase. When the appropriations bill for fiscal 1954 was passed, distributive education was again restricted to $450,000. The following year, however, distributive education was raised to $900,000 and in 1956 to $1,500,000.[7]

The Establishment of the Department of Health, Education, and Welfare

On April 11, 1953, the Department of Health, Education, and Welfare was organized with cabinet status. This came about as the result of the congressional acceptance of President Dwight Eisenhower's government reorganization plan, which was substantially the same as the plan submitted twice previously by Harry Truman. This time, however, Congress chose to approve it. For the first time since 1939, the United States Office of Education was a part of an agency with cabinet status. As the Office of Education administered the federal participation in vocational education, those in vocational education were hopeful that they would have a greater influence upon the creation of the administration's policy on vocational education. And the proposed increase by the Bureau of the Budget for distributive education in fiscal year 1954 indicates that proponents of vocational education, both in and out of government, were making their presence known.[8]

National Defense Education Act

Several changes in federal policy toward vocational education occurred in the mid and late 1950s. In 1956, Congress approved the use of federal funds to aid vocational programs involved in the training of practical nurses. This was a part of the Health Amendments Act of 1956—PL 84-911—and it amended the George-Barden Act by authorizing an additional $5 million per year for five years to train practical nurses. This authorization known as Title II of the George-Barden Act was later extended for two additional years and then became a permanent authorization in 1963. Also in 1956, Congress approved a second amendment to the George-Barden Act. This amendment, which passed after much debate, established a permanent authorization of $550,000 to train professional personnel needed in commercial fishing. The funds were to be administered by the Department of Interior and required no state or local matching funds. However, Congress did not appropriate any of these authorization funds until fiscal year 1963.[9]

The most important development of this period for vocational education was the passage of the National Defense Education Act of 1958. In the fall of 1957, the Soviet Union placed the first man-made satellite, "sputnik," in orbit around the earth. Suddenly Congress and the public became aware of what educators and educational critics had been warning of for years. American education was not producing the quantity of highly talented and skilled persons in the sciences and related vital fields necessary to keep pace with advancing technology. Within a year after "sputnik," Congress attempted to remedy the problem by passing the National Defense Education Act of 1958—the NDEA. As passed and signed into law (PL 85-864), the NDEA proposed to spend $1 billion in the following four years to produce the needed scientists and technicians and to improve the general quality of American education. The act was divided into ten separate titles or sections. Probably the most commonly known is Title II, which provided for loans to college students majoring in science, mathematics, engineering, or modern languages. Students majoring in elementary or secondary education with the intent to teach in these areas were also eligible for the loans. For those who became teachers, 50 percent of their loans could be canceled at the rate of 10 percent per year if they remained in the profession for at least five years. Title II of NDEA financed the college education of virtually legions of students during the late 1950s and 1960s.[10]

However, the section that was important to vocational education was Title VIII known as the Area Vocational Education Programs. This section amended the George-Barden Act of 1946 by becoming Title III of that Act. Thus, the funds appropriated under its provisions were subject to the same restrictions and requirements as all other funds authorized by the George-Barden Act. Title VIII of NDEA authorized annual appropriations of $15 million for the following four years. These funds were to be matched by the state and used to train persons for highly skilled technical occupations that were recognized as vital to the national defense and requiring scientific knowledge. The programs offered under this provision ranged from computer programming and nuclear engineering to aircraft mechanics. Another provision was that Title VIII funds had to be used for less than college grade programs. Some states that had previously established area vocational schools used the funds to finance technical courses in these schools. Other states used this opportunity to establish area vocational schools to train high-school and posthigh-school-age persons in skilled occupations. Title VIII of NDEA was extended until 1963 when it was made a permanent authorization.[11]

The Impact of John F. Kennedy

Vocational Education and a Changing Society

The nature of work and life in America changed as the levels of science and technology advanced. However, after 1957 the pace of change in technology was greatly accelerated. Technology developed so quickly that job changes and living styles were sorely pressed to keep up. Technology in the form of automation ended the jobs of thousands of workers. An often-cited example is that in the late 1950s the introduction of the automatic elevator in New York City put forty thousand elevator operators out of work.[12]

The impact of changing technology was not limited to the unskilled jobs. Those in the semiskilled, skilled, and professional areas also felt the changes. New machinery reduced employment in the coal fields from four hundred fifteen thousand in 1950 to one hundred thirty-six thousand by 1962. From 1956 to the early 1960s, the construction industry grew by 32 percent— while construction jobs declined by 24 percent. The Bureau of the Census employed four thousand statisticians to tabulate and interpret the 1950 Census. With new automated equipment, the 1960 Census required only fifty statisticians.[13]

Whereas technology ended old jobs, it also created new ones. The new jobs, however, required different skills and—in many cases—greater technical knowledge. It was easier for those workers with better educational preparation and a greater amount of financial resources to be successfully retrained for these newer and more technical jobs. Those workers with inadequate educational and technical preparation—usually in the unskilled and semiskilled groups—found it difficult if not impossible to be successfully retrained. By the early 1960s, the nation was in a paradoxical situation. Unemployment and poverty increased as thousands lost their jobs to technological advances. At the same time, thousands of jobs were unfilled because of the shortage of workers with the needed technical skills necessary to hold the jobs.[14]

Whereas the problems of increasing unemployment and a growing shortage of trained workers were important socioeconomic developments for Americans, an equally important change was taking place in the basic philosophy of the nation. As the problems grew in magnitude, it became increasingly obvious that the individual American was becoming less able to control his or her destiny. Such problems of unemployment coupled with the higher training requirements for the newer jobs meant that for many the loss of a job found them unable to obtain either a new job or the training necessary for a new job. By 1960 most Americans realized that the federal government would have to furnish the leadership necessary to reconcile unemployment with the shortage of workers.[15]

Vocational Education Reexamined

In the early 1950s a movement began to reexamine the role of vocational education in America. While those involved in vocational education and a few other interested persons discussed its role, little outside attention was given until the sputnik. In the late 1950s, the interest in vocational education grew. Federal aid to vocational education was increased through the practical nurses program, the fisheries program, and the National Defense Education Act. These programs were heavily slanted toward the scientific and technically oriented areas—the special, highly skilled, technical, and scientific jobs. The equally important but less scientifically oriented technical jobs and the service occupations were relegated to a secondary position under these programs.By 1960 there was a growing concern for and an increasing recognition of the need for vocational training programs in these areas. Unless vocational education moved to include these occupations in its structure, it would fail in its effort to keep pace with the changing demands of the job market.[16]

Distributive Education Reexamined

While the importance of vocational education in general was being reexamined, the position of distributive education was also under reevaluation. Throughout the late 1950s and early 1960s, there developed a growing realization that merchandising and marketing would become more and more important as the demand for consumer goods increased. Educators, government agencies, and business organizations agreed by the early 1960s that in the decades ahead the distributive occupations would require an increasing number of workers with higher levels of training and education. It was urged that training programs for store employees be continued and strengthened. The most important consensus was that the preemployment and cooperative training programs in distributive education for those of high school age should be expanded. The combination of classroom instruction and work experience was deemed by most as the best method of producing competent qualified store workers. Such workers, it was also believed, would be the ones most qualified and most likely to advance into management positions.[17]

Manpower Programs

By the early 1960s, the need for vocational training and retraining was critical in certain areas of the country. In May 1961 the Congress passed the Area Redevelopment Act (P.L. 87-27). This act authorized an annual appropriation of $4.5 million until 1965. The funds were to be used to finance the vocational training of eligible persons living in the areas designated as economically distressed. The state agencies, with the approval of the secretary of labor, were to determine who was eligible and what program was needed. The Department of Health, Education, and Welfare contracted a local school district to establish the program and conduct the training. And, the federal government financed the entire operation.[18]

In March 1962 the basic concept of the Area Redevelopment Act was applied to the entire nation through the Manpower Development and Training Act (P.L. 87–415). This act recognized the need to provide a system for training the unemployed and retraining those whose jobs had been eliminated through technological advancements. Title I of the act directs the secretary of labor to study the needs and requirements in the areas of manpower development and report to the president. For this purpose, an appropriation of $2 million was authorized for fiscal year 1963.

The authorization was increased to $3 million per year for fiscal years 1964, 1965, and 1966. Title II authorized the training of workers for those jobs revealed by the Title I studies as available. This title was amended to authorize an appropriation of $97 million for the fiscal year 1963, $161 million for 1964, $407 million for 1965, and $281 million for 1966. In 1965, the title was amended to authorize $454 million for 1966 and to require the states to finance 10 percent of the costs after June 30, 1966.[19]

Although the Congress authorized appropriations for the ARA and MDTA, the actual amounts appropriated fell short of those authorized. For example, the legislation authorized appropriations of $4.5 million for ARA and $97 million for MDTA for fiscal year 1963. The actual appropriations for that year were less than $2.5 million for ARA and $20 million for MDTA.[20]

During the first year of the MDTA and its programs, it became evident that unless the format of the MDTA was changed it would not be able to ease the problems of unemployment. Society was changing and the newly developed jobs were becoming more and more technical. Such occupations required the mastery of fundamental educational skills, and those who most needed the opportunities offered by MDTA—the hard-core unemployed—were the most poorly educated segment of American society. MDTA programs were available only to those whose educational background was sufficient to make them readily trainable for existing jobs. Thus, educational deficiencies kept most of the hard-core unemployed from qualifying for the programs. One estimate was that more than one-third of the unemployed had not completed an eighth-grade education. Of those who qualified for the MDTA programs, only 10 percent had not completed the eighth grade. During 1963, 60 percent of the MDTA trainees had completed a twelfth-grade education. But, among the unempolyed, from among whom the trainees were selected, the percentage of those who had completed high school was about 40 percent. During its first year, the MDTA tapped only the highest educational level in the pool of unemployed. The illiterate and semiliterate were, for the most part, untouched by MDTA.[21]

In December 1963, Congress amended the MDTA. Among these amendments were two of importance. First, the secretary of labor was provided with the authority to certify individuals for as much as twenty weeks of basic education. It was hoped that this remedial education would decrease the educational deficiencies of these individuals to the point that they could be successfully trained. Second, the original act stipulated that no more than 5 percent of the MDTA funds could be spent on out-of-school youths under the age of nineteen. The amendment authorized a maximum of 25 percent that could be spent on youths under the age of twenty-two.[22]

Report of the President's Panel On Vocational Education

President John F. Kennedy was greatly concerned about the state of American education—both traditional and vocational. In a message to the Congress on American Education, February 20, 1961, President Kennedy stated that the rapidly changing technology of the times made a reevaluation of the federal legislation concerning vocational education necessary before additional programs were established and funds allocated. He directed the secretary of health, education, and welfare to appoint an advisory body to study the national vocational education acts, evaluate their accomplishments, and assess the needs of the future. After a delay, it was announced on October 5, 1961, that the Panel of Consultants on Vocational Education had been appointed and was ready to undertake the task. The panel consisted of twenty-five members representing nearly every section of the nation. The panel flected the diversity of the economy with representatives from agriculture, industry, business, labor, and education. The chairman of the panel was Dr. Benjamin C. Willis, the general superintendent of schools of Chicago, Illinois. The panel organized its staff and began work on November 9, 1961. It completed its assignment and submitted its report a year later, November 27, 1962.[23]

The panel developed a series of general recommendations that concerned needs of the future and what vocational education must do to meet those needs. The panel believed that vocational education must:

> Offer training opportunities to the 21 million noncollege graducates who will enter the labor market in the 1960's.

> Provide training or retraining for the millions of workers whose skills and technical knowledge must be updated, as well as those whose jobs will disappear due to increasing efficiency, automation, or economic change.

> Meet the critical need for highly skilled craftsmen and technicians through education during and after the high school years.

Expand vocational and technical training programs consistent with employment possibilities and national economic needs.

Make educational opportunities equally available to all, regardless of race, sex, scholastic aptitude, or place of residence.[24]

The panel had specific recommendations concerning vocational education. It urged that the local-state-federal cooperation increase its support of vocational and technical training in five areas. First, the panel urged increased support for high-school students who were preparing to enter the job market. One specific recommendation in this area was that preemployment training in the distributive occupations be made eligible for federal financial support. Second, the panel recommended that highly individualized training be made available for those high-school-age youths with handicaps—academic, socioeconomic, or other types. Third, the panel urged the federal government to increase its support of full-time, post-high-school vocational and technical training. This would include the training of both adults and those just out of high school. Fourth, the panel recommended that part-time, short-term training courses for youth and adults be expanded. This would include both those unemployed and those with jobs. The panel believed that with the constantly and rapidly changing technology, such short courses would allow workers to update their skills or acquire new ones. This would allow them to keep their jobs or get new ones if the old jobs were eliminated by technological changes. Fifth, the panel urged changes in the services and facilities to assure quality in the technical and vocational programs. Among these were improvement of training programs for vocational teachers, the orientation of basic education materials to the specific occupation covered by each training program, the availability of occupational information and guidance for all students, and an increase in and a national coordination of research pertaining to vocational and technical education. The panel issued one last recommendation concerning funding. It advised that the federal vocational budget for the 1963–64 school year should be $400 million.[25]

Vocational Education Act of 1963

Passage of the Act

Based upon the recommendations of the Panel of Consultants on Vocational Education, the administration drafted an omnibus bill for vocational education. This bill was introduced as S. 580 and H.R. 3000. Basically it followed the suggestions of the panel, which included the elimination of features connected with the Smith-Hughes and George-Barden Acts. Early in 1963 it appeared that the administration's bill was in trouble. At that point, Representative Carl D. Perkins of Kentucky introduced H.R. 4955. This bill kept some features of the administration's bill but substituted its own language for Part V of H.R. 3000—it maintained the provisions of Smith-Hughes and George-Barden Acts. Also H.R. 4955 had been drafted as a substitute by the American Vocational Association and thus was acceptable to most of those involved in vocational education. H.R. 4955 passed the House on August 6 by a vote of 378 to 21, and passed the Senate on October 8 by a vote of 80 to 4. Since the revisions passed by the House and Senate were different, the bill spent the following two months in a conference committee. Agreement was reached on December 13 and on December 18, 1963, President Lyndon B. Johnson signed H.R. 4955 into law as P.L. 88-210.[26]

Provisions of the Vocational Education Act of 1963

The Vocational Education Act of 1963 authorized appropriations in the amount of $60 million for fiscal 1964, $118.5 million for fiscal 1965, $177.5 million for fiscal 1966, and $225.5 million for each year thereafter. Ninety percent of the funds were to be allocated to the states on the basis of their population in various age groups in need of vocational training. And, a minimum of 3 percent of each state's allotment must be spent on activities designed to improve the quality of vocational education, such as teacher education, supervisory training, and program evaluations. Also, a minimum of one-third of each state's allotment for the period ending July 1, 1968, and a minimum of 25 percent in each subsequent year was to be used for full-time post-high-school training, or the construction of area vocational school, or both. With these proscriptions in mind, the states were authorized to spend their allocations for:

(1) Vocational education for persons attending high school;
(2) Vocational education for persons who have completed or left high school and who are available for full-time study in preparation for entering the labor market;
(3) Vocational education for persons (other than persons who are receiving training allowances under the Manpower Development and Training Act of 1962 (Public Law 87-415), the Area Redevelopment Act (Public Law 87-27), or the Trade Expansion Act

of 1962 (Public Law 87-794) who have already entered the labor market and who need training or retraining to achieve stability or advancement in employment;

(4) Vocational education for persons who have academic, socioeconomic, or other handicaps that prevent them from succeeding in the regular vocational education program;

(5) Construction of Area vocational education school facilities;

(6) Ancillary services and activities to assure quality in all vocational education programs, such as teacher training and supervision, program evaluation, special demonstration and experimental programs, development of instructional materials, and State administration and leadership, including periodic evaluation of State and local vocational education programs and services in light of information regarding current and projected manpower needs and job opportunities.[27]

The Vocational Education Act of 1963 also allowed for the establishment of experimental, residential, vocational education school offering programs of four years' duration, aid to vocational student work-study programs, the expansion of agricultural training programs to include agricultural related jobs that did not involve the actual tilling of the soil, the expansion of home economics programs to include related but nonhomemaking jobs which might be available, the development of preemployment training in distributive occupations, the extension on a permanent basis of Title II of the George-Barden Act—training in practical nursing, and, the limited extension of the National Defense Education Act, Public Law 815, and Public Law 874.[28]

Changes in Policy under the Vocational Education Act of 1963

Several changes in basic federal policy toward vocational education were part of the Vocational Education Act of 1963. While continuing the programs and the authorization of funds established by the Smith-Hughes and George-Barden Acts, the act of 1963 amended the previous legislation to allow states greater flexibility in how the Smith-Hughes and George-Barden funds were used. The Smith-Hughes and George-Barden Acts required that set percentages of the funds had to be spent for required programs such as those in agriculture, trade and industry, and home economics. Under the new law, states could divert funds previously earmarked for one area, such as agriculture or home economics, into another area in which studies indicated a need for more workers, such as industry or distributive occupations.

The only restrictions upon the state was that first it must produce evidence that such a transfer of funds was in the best interest of the state and then receive the approval of the U.S. commissioner of education. By creating the machinery for such a transfer of funds, the federal government recognized that job availability varied with the growth of population, economic development, and technical advances. This provision allowed the states to adjust their vocational programs in the effort to keep pace with these changes.[29]

Of equal importance was the decision of the federal government through the act of 1963 to grant continuing support to the concept of area vocational schools and to provide funds for their construction. Also the willingness of the government to allow research and experimentation in vocational matters was notable. The establishment of the experimental four-year resident vocational schools and demonstration programs were evidence of the government's new interest in improving vocational training. The authorization of funds for training persons with academic, socioeconomic, and other handicaps reflected an important redirection of federal policy. The overall effect of the Vocational Education Act of 1963 was a recognition by the federal government that vocational education must be a vital segment of the educational system of the nation. In fact, there were educators, both in general and vocational education, who hailed the act of 1963 as something of an equal rights act for vocational education.[30]

The authors of the Vocational Education Act of 1963 also recognized the need for periodic review of the federal policy on vocational training. The law required the secretary of health, education, and welfare to appoint in 1966 a twelve-member panel—known as the Advisory Council of Vocational Education—to review the federal programs and to submit its report no later than January 1, 1968. After that, the act required the secretary to appoint new councils to review federal programs at intervals not to exceed five years. The Vocational Education Act of 1963 thus contained a built-in review system in the effort to keep federal programs and policies current with the reality of the vocational needs of the nation.[31]

By early 1966 the Vocational Education Act of 1963 was being hailed for its catalytic effect on vocational education. Enrollment had grown from an annual rate of 4 percent in the years preceding the act to 14 percent a year following its enactment. By 1966 enrollment in vocational education in the United States numbered 6,070,059. Federal expenditure for vocational education rose from $55 million in 1964 to $234 million in 1966. Approximately 125 area vocational schools were under construction during 1965 in accordance with the act and over 200 more were in the planning stage. Furthermore, those who praised the act noted that even with the numerous programs that were financed entirely by federal funds or which received 90 percent of their funds from federal sources, the state and local authorities were still providing $2 to every federal dollar spent for vocational education. In the years following the approval of the Vocational Education Act of 1963, the impact of the expanded federal programs was easily seen. A survey conducted in 1967 for the Advisory Council on Vocational education contacted 109 local schools. These schools reported that 683 new vocational programs had been started since the passage of the act. New buildings, new programs, and new federal money—the most important of the three—were the changes wrought by the Act of 1963.[32]

Effects of the Vocational Education Act of 1963 on Distributive Education

The impact of the Vocational Education Act of 1963 on distributive education was dramatic. Enrollment in distributive training programs increased by nearly 26 percent from 1964 (334,126) to 1966 (420,426), and the ratio of full-time students (high school) to part-time students (adults) increased for 17.3 percent in 1964 to 27.8 percent in 1966. In most cases the increase was the result of the greater infusion of federal funds into the distributive programs. The money and the new regulation that allowed preemployment training to be funded created the increased enrollment in the programs. The states intensified their efforts in the established programs, and they began new preparatory programs.[33]

Under the George-Barden Act, it was difficult for smaller schools to qualify a distributive education program for federal aid. The school had to be located in a trade area of sufficient size to allow the students the opportunity to obtain the required part-time employment. Under the new regulations, these smaller schools could offer preemployment training without the mandatory work experience. These new programs provided the students with the classroom knowledge of the occupation and gave them a certain amount of saleable skills. Not only did the new preemployment programs serve the smaller schools, they also provided those students who were interested in the concept of a liberal education an opportunity to acquire merchandising skills without sacrificing the time allocated to their traditional subjects. Thus, these courses also drew students who wished to acquire a basic understanding of the occupations before they went on into college or other fields.[34]

As important as the high school programs were, they did not constitute the mass of the increased enrollment for the period. From 1965 to 1966, 71.6 percent of the increased enrollment was in the adult programs. As with the high school programs, the new money, preemployment courses, and new regulations drew students to the programs.[35]

The War on Poverty and the Economic Opportunity Act of 1964

On August 20, 1964, President Lyndon Johnson signed the antipoverty bill (S.2642) into law as PL 88-452—better known as the Economic Opportunity Act of 1964. Whereas the goal of the act was to improve the econimic status of the poor, part of this was to be accomplished through job training and work experience. Among the provisions of the act was the establishment of the Neighborhood Youth Corps and the Job Corps, both of which were intended to provide jobs, training, and income to youths from low-income homes. These were not new ideas. A movement had started in the late 1950s to establish a Youth Conservation Corps patterned after the Civilian Conservation Corps of the New Deal era. This movement was stalled as it either failed to gain the backing of the administration or the approval of Congress. The Economic Opportunity Act of 1964 contained adaptations of many of the earlier proposals for such a youth corps.[36]

As established under the act of 1964, the Neighborhood Youth Corps was to provide work experience and income for unemployed youth aged sixteen to twenty-one—both those in and those out of school. It was assumed that through this program the youth would gain skills and experience that would increase their opportunities for future employment. Also, it was hoped that the income they received from this employment would allow and encourage them to continue their education.[37]

The Job Corps was established to provide training for those unemployed, untrained youths aged sixteen to twenty-one whose major obstacle to receiving adequate education, training, and employment was the environment of their home. The Job Corps offered such young people a two-year work-training program through a series of regional centers. At these centers, the time was to be divided between education, training, and public service work. The parentage of the Job Corps was evident through the stipulation requiring that 40 percent of the enrollees be assigned to the Youth Conservation Corps. This unit was under the direction of the U.S Forest Service and the National Parks Service. Its work assignments were conservation and natural resources projects selected by the services.[38]

In most cases the Neighborhood Youth Corps and the Job Corps were handled in the same general way as the regular vocational education programs. With the exception of some conservation centers in the Job Corps, the remaining programs were initiated and organized by the local and state authorities. The federal government assumed the financial responsibility for the programs. Although these programs were not vocational education in its traditional sense, the intent was to provide a limited amount of job training coupled with work experience. It was a double-edged effort by the federal government to provide a degree of job training to those who otherwise might not be able to obtain it, and to provide a limited amount of additional income to the segment of the population that needed it the most.[39]

Vocational Educational Amendments of 1968

Report of the Advisory Council on Vocational Education: 1968

In accordance with the provisions of the Vocational Education Act of 1963, an Advisory Council on Vocational Education was appointed in November 1966. By law, this twelve-member council—chaired by Martin W. Essex, the superintendent for Public Instruction for the State of Ohio—was required to evaluate the federal vocational programs, assess the implementation of the Act of 1963, and make recommendations for improvement. The council worked for a year and submitted its report in December 1967.[40]

The council made twenty-six recommendations for changes in the federal vocational education program. Taken together, these recommendations called for a complete overhaul of the federal legislation governing the programs. However, two of the recommendations were of greater importance than the others. One called for the combining of all federal vocational legislation into one manageable act, which would eliminate the Smith-Hughes, the George-Barden, and other acts which carried their own specific regulations and earmarked funds. Under this proposal, all vocational programs would be under one act with one set of regulations. A second recommendation called for an open-ended authorization of over $1.5 billion a year for vocational education. The Council urged that these funds be allocated in the following manner: grants to States—$500 million; Work-Study Program—$350 million; Innovative Programs—$200 million; Residential Vocational Schools—$200 million; Program for Socially, Economically, and Culturally Disadvantaged—$300 million; Vocational Homemaking—$15 million. These two of the twenty-six recommendations created a great deal of interest among those in vocational education. However, it was the proposed $1.5 billion per year that interested them the most.[41]

Among the other recommendations were the creation of a cabinet-level Department of Education and Manpower Development to administer the vocational and manpower programs, to establish a permanent authority for work study and work experience programs in the secondary schools and those in postsecondary programs related to vocational and technical education, to permit the matching of the federal allotment on a statewide basis rather than on the basis of each individual program, and to establish of a pilot project known as the Learning Corps to provide improved learning experiences for economically disadvantaged youths.[42]

Provisions of the Amendments

Early in 1968, bills were introduced into Congress that were based upon the recommendations of the council. While several people were listed as sponsors of the bills, the prime movers of the House bill were Representative Roman C. Pucinski of Illinois and Representative Lloyd Meeds of Washington. Senator Wayne Morse of Oregon was the main supporter of the Senate bill. The House approved H.R. 18366 on July 15 and the Senate passed its revision (S.3770) by a vote of 88 to 0 on July 17. A conference committee was organized and the proposal remained in conference until early October. At that time the Senate accepted most of the House bill and passed it on October 2. The House approved it the following day and President Johnson signed it into law as PL 90–576 on October 16, 1968.[43]

The Vocational Education Amendments of 1968 (PL 90-576)

followed some but not all of the recommendations made by the Advisory Council on Vocational Education. It did unify all federal vocational legislation under one act by repealing the provisions of several acts including the amendments to the Smith-Hughes Act, the earmarking of funds under Smith-Hughes, and the repeal of the George-Barden Act. It did not, however, authorize the suggested annual appropriations of $1.5 billion. The act authorized an appropriation for grants to the states for general programs and training of $355 million for fiscal year 1969, $565 million in fiscal year 1970, $675 million in fiscal year 1971 and 1972, and $565 million for fiscal year 1973 and each year thereafter. The act also authorized funds for specific programs through fiscal year 1972. These additional funds brought the total annual authorization for vocational education to $542 million for fiscal year 1969, $857.5 million for fiscal year 1970, $870 million for fiscal year 1971, and $910 million for fiscal year 1972. Unless continued by new legislation, the total annual appropriation would drop to $565 million for fiscal year 1973. By the fourth year under the act, the total authorization would still be more than $500 million under the recommended $1.5 billion. However, this was a considerable overall increase in authorizations.[44]

As has been previously noted, actual appropriations do not necessarily follow the authorized amounts. The appropriations for vocational purposes during fiscal year 1969 and fiscal year 1972 are typical examples. The total authorized for fiscal year 1969 was $542 million, but the actual amount appropriated was $248,216,000. For fiscal year 1972, the authorized amount was $910 million. However, the actual appropriation was slightly more than $569 million.[45]

Among the remainder of the provisions in the Vocational Education Amendments of 1968 were the establishment and/or short-term continuation of special programs for the disadvantaged and handicapped, special grants for curriculum development and staff training, and consumer education. The act also required the states to submit state plans for vocational education with a five-year projection included. These plans could be amended by the states. The act also gave the U.S. commissioner of education the power, for the first time, to disapprove any portion of a state plan and withhold the appropriate federal funds from those programs.[46]

Another change included in the Amendments of 1968 was the establishment of state and national advisory councils for vocational education. Under this provision no state was eligible for federal funds unless its state plan had been drawn up with the participation of its State Advisory Council. Such a council must represent various levels of educational institutions and administrations. Also its membership must include individuals who were familiar with the problems of manpower development, disadvantaged students, and vocational education. These councils were required to hold at least one open hearing each year devoted to testimony from the public concerning the views of private citizens on vocational education.[47]

The National Advisory Council on Vocational Education was to consist of twenty-one members appointed by the president to staggered three-year terms. The council must include representatives of labor and management. Its membership must include those with knowledge of the various occupations, the problems of manpower programs, the workings of state and local vocational programs, and the problems of the poor and disadvantaged. The law requires that the council meet a minimum of four times per year. It was to submit an annual report concerning the state of vocational education and include in it its recommendations for improvement.[48]

The Vocational Education Amendments of 1968 provided an additional stimulus for vocational education. The amendments followed the same general guidelines as the Vocational Education Act of 1963, while continuing and strengthening its provisions. The amendments represented the continued commitment of Congress to vocational education and the realization that adjustments between traditional and vocational education were necessary. The amendments of 1968 were considered the first step in equalizing the dual educational systems of the nation.[49]

Vocational Education Amendments of 1972 and 1976

The Vocational Education Act of 1963 was amended a second time in 1972. In that year, the vocational amendments were part of a larger educational package known as the Education Amendments of 1972–P.L. 92–318. Among the provisions that applied to vocational education were those extending some of the programs of the amendments of 1968 through June 30, 1976. In particular, this included the Exemplary Programs and Projects and the provisions of Consumer and Homemaking Education. Also the amendments of 1972 authorized the establishment of a Bureau of Occupational and Adult Education. This bureau would be under the Office of Education and would be headed by a deputy commissioner of education qualified in the fields of vocational and occupational education.[50]

In October 1976, President Gerald Ford signed into law the Educational Amendments of 1976—P.L. 94-482. Title II of this act contained the amendments to the Vocational Education Act of 1963. First, it extended the funding and programs established under the Act of 1963 and the amendments of 1968 and 1972 through fiscal year 1977. Second, it provided a means for a smooth transition to the new provisions that become effective during fiscal year 1978. These included a greater involvement of the public and of state agencies in the development of vocational policy for each state, the designation of one agency in each state that will be solely responsible for administering the vocational policies of that state, programs to end sex discrimination and sex stereotyping in state vocational programs, and a greater emphasis on vocational guidance and counciling. The funds authorized under this act were to increase from a total just under $1.1 billion for fiscal year 1978 to slightly more than $1.7 billion in fiscal year 1982.[51]

Criticism of Vocational Education in the 1970s

HEW Report of 1972

During the early and mid 1970s, two reports concerning vocational education were released by the Department of Health, Education, and Welfare and by the General Accounting Office. These reports were highly critical of vocational education, its achievements, and its expenditures. The first report was authorized in 1971 by Secretary of Health, Education, and Welfare Elliot L. Richardson, and completed and submitted in 1972. The report, titled *Work in America*, contained 262 pages, which less than thirty pages dealt with education and only four pages with vocational education. The report was mainly concerned with the nature and quality of work. Its major contention was that work was no longer a satisfying experience for many Americans because job development had not kept up with the rising expectations and the increasing educational background of the workers. The techniques of mass production had reduced work to boredom with little worker responsibility and almost no pride in accomplishment.[52]

This general decline in the value and satisfying quality of work led to the criticism of vocational education in the report. "Vocational education in the high schools has failed to give students useful skills or place them in satisfying jobs."[53] Specifically the report charged that (1) over half of the high school vocational graduates did not take their first job within the area of their training, (2) that the unemployment figures for high school vocational graduates were not significantly different from those for nonvocational high school graduates, (3) that the unemployment figures were higher for high school vocational graduates than for graduates of other vocational schools—junior college and postsecondary programs, (4) that high school vocational curriculum was the most expensive form of education costing 50 percent to 75 percent more than any other high school curricula, and (5) that the high school programs teach the older, established, and accepted jobs and skills. The report charged that in a rapidly changing technology such jobs may be obsolete within a few years of the student's graduation.[54]

These few pages of the report aroused the wrath of vocational educators. In May 1973, Dr. Po-yen Koo of the New Jersey Department of Education published a well-written rebuttal in the *American Vocational Journal*. Dr. Koo charged that the report was inadequately researched, poorly written, and biased. There was a degree of validity to his charges. He demonstrated that quotations were taken out of context and misinterpreted. In general, he showed that the vocational section of the report was not in the tradition of good scholarship. Dr. Koo cited studies and statistics that refuted the claims of the report concerning high school vocational graduates and unemployment. He also refuted the charges of the report concerning high school vocational graduates and wage-earning ability. However, Dr. Koo's masterfully written rebuttal did not approach the questions of (1) if the goal of vocational education is to provide the student with training for earning and if over half of the graduates did not take employment in the areas of their training, is it accomplishing its goal?, and (2) if the cost of the high school vocational curricula is actually 50 percent to 75 percent greater than any other is it a sound financial investment when less than half of the graduates find employment in their areas of training?[55]

GAO Report of 1975

On December 31, 1974, the General Accounting Office submitted to Congress its report concerning the expenditure of federal funds for vocational education. The GAO began its preliminary work for the report in 1972 and started the major part of the investigation in late 1973. The report examined how funds provided under Part B of the Vocational Education Act of 1963 and the Amendments of 1968 were spent in seven states—California, Kentucky, Minnesota, Ohio, Pennsylvania, Texas, and Washington. These states were selected for the audit because of their diverse vocational programs and between them they accounted for 30 percent of the federal funds spent in fiscal 1973—$146 million out of a total of $482 million.[56]

The report listed over forty findings and made recommendations to Congress and to the secretary of health, education, and welfare on most of them. In particular, the GAO charged first that it was the historical intent of Congress for the federal funds to be used as a catalyst to encourage the establishment of vocational programs by state and local authorities. The GAO believed that too great a percentage of the federal funds was being used to maintain established programs when it should be used to expand programs and create new ones. Second, the GAO contended that too much of the federal funds (16%) were being held on the state level for administrative and supportive activities. It charged that in some states the percentage was as high as 22 percent. Third, the GAO charged that too often the states rather than effectively using existing facilities opted to use available federal funds and build new vocational buildings. The GAO believed that this was not the intention of the legislation in providing funds for area vocational schools.[57]

As with *Work in America*, the GAO report kindled the ire of the vocational administrators and educators. The charge that the sample used by the GAO was too small to have national implications was leveled at the report. Those making this charge contended that although the report covered 30 percent of the funds spent that year, the selection of seven states was not sufficient for such an audit. The GAO responded with a statement that modern theories of sampling and statistics supported their sample selection.[58]

One director of a state vocational system answered the three major charges of the GAO in an article published in the *American Vocational Journal*. Dr. Carl F. Lamar of Kentucky argued that (1) the use of federal funds for maintenance of existing programs was within the intent of the Vocational Education Act of 1963, (2) that the purely administrative costs at the state level actually averaged less than 9 percent, and (3) that the Vocational Education Act of 1963 emphasized the creation of area vocational schools and provided the funds for construction. Whereas Dr. Lamar defended vocational education, the difference between the GAO charges and his rebuttal came down to an interpretation of what was the intent of the law and what constituted an acceptable level of expenditures. Dr. Lamar's position maintained that vocational education was within the letter of the law. The GAO questioned the intent and the need for certain expenditures.[59]

Career Education

The concept that children need to begin their exploration of the world of work at an early age has been discussed by theorists since the turn of the century. In its annual report for 1969, the National Advisory Council on Vocational Education urged changes in the curriculum of the elementary schools to provide students with the opportunity to study jobs. The council contended that early education would give the student a better perspective on occupations and would develop respect for work and pride in accomplishment. The council recommended the expenditure of vocational funds to develop such a curriculum, train teachers, and establish pilot programs.[60]

In 1971 this concept of exploring the world of work was given a new name by Dr. Sidney P. Marland, Jr., the United States commissioner of education. Dr. Marland applied the name "career education" to this concept and became its most avid proponent. As envisioned by Marland, career education would start in the first grade and continue through the twelfth grade and beyond. All students would take the career education curricula, and the student would possess the basic job skills that were necessary for employment upon his leaving school. According to his basic plan, the student would examine basic occupation types during grades one through six. In the seventh and eighth grades, the student would begin to concentrate on those particular job clusters that interested him. In the ninth and tenth grades, the student would narrow his job interest, do some in-depth study of his choices, visit work places, try some of the basic skills needed, and in general get the feel of what it would be like to do this type of work. In the eleventh and twelfth grades, the student would select a job type and begin to learn the skills needed for that occupation. Upon graduation, the student would be prepared to enter the world of work, or if his chosen area required further study—technical school, junior college, or university training—the experience gained through career education would better prepare the student for his studies and for work after completing the additional training. Marland backed up his convictions by assigning a large part of the Office of Education's discretionary funds to pilot projects in career education established in six school districts—Mesa, Arizona; Los Angeles, California; Jefferson County, Colorado; Atlanta, Georgia; Pontiac, Michigan; and Hackensack, New Jersey.[61].

Career education became a highly popular educational concept. Within a few months after Marland began his campaign of support, numerous theorists and educators were advocating career education. Congress became interested in the concept and on August 21, 1974, passed Public Law 93-389 of which Section 406 dealt with career education. This section stated the philosophy of Congress toward career education and authorized the U.S. commissioner of education to use certain federal funds to aid the states in developing curriculum for career education. Authorizations for $15 million annually were passed for 1975 and 1976. However, only $10 million were actually appropriated in each of these years. The Educational Amendments of 1976 (P.L. 94-482) also contained a section concerning career education. Congress also authorized $10 million for fiscal 1978 to be used to create state plans for career education.[62]

Public Law 93-380 (1974) established within the Office of Education an Office of Career Education, which was to be headed by a director who reported directly to the U.S Commissioner of Education. Also included in P.L. 93-280 was a provision for a National Advisory Council for Career Education. The council was to consist of twelve appointed members selected by the secretary of health, education, and welfare. These members were to be drawn from the public and would constitute the voting membership of the council. Nine additional nonvoting members would represent concerned federal agencies named in the act.[63]

When the Advisory Council was established, Dr. Marland—who had left the Office of Education for private employment—was appointed chairman. Through the summer and fall of 1975, Marland and others developed a legislative proposal concerning career education. In December 1975, Representative Carl D. Perkins of Kentucky introduced into the House a bill based upon this draft. In December 1977, a revised version of this bill was enacted as the Career Education Incentive Act of 1977. This legislation provided federal funds to implement a nationwide program of career education.[64]

Career education was readily integrated into the educational philosophy of most administrators and teachers of vocational subjects. In fact, the digest of the 1975 reports of State Advisory Councils on Vocational Education noted that career education was so well accepted that most of the discussion of it concerned how to speed up its establishment:

> There appears to be a remarkably strong, widespread perception that career education is the natural and necessary context for vocational education. The Council reports reflected little need to discuss the merits of career education; rather, many Councils call for increased funding and state leadership to accelerate its full implementation.[65]

Career education is not without its critics. Skepticism concerning the concept and the probable degree of its implementation have been voiced on several occasions. The HEW report *Work in America*, which was released in 1972, argued that if career education were modeled after traditional vocational education, it would not succeed. The report contended that any educational curriculum that turns out students oriented to a single career does not serve the best interest of the students. This opinion was based on the extremely mobile state that exists in the present-day job market as a result of rapidly changing technology. Basically, the report favored the first part of Dr. Marland's plan for career education. It viewed that the most important contribution which career education could make was the creation of an understanding on the part of the student concerning the nature of work. The report praised the study of job types and the use of field trips on the elementary school level as a means to understand work. The authors of *Work in America* argued that career education could be a valuable concept as long as it was used to expose the student to the world of work and did not try to teach him a single marketable skill.[66]

The argument concerning the purpose of career education, which is a rerun of the age-old arguments between liberal education and vocational training, continued to appear in the journals into 1977. Should career education prepare the student in a marketable skill for employment or, should it be a broad-based humanistic education designed to give the student an understanding of work? Should it prepare the student for a job or, should it prepare him for work? The arguments concerning the purpose of career education are in reality the latest phase in the debate between the vocational and liberal philosophies of education.[67]

However, the popularity of vocational education among the students continued to grow. In the years between 1966 and 1974, the total nationwide enrollment in vocational education more than doubled, from 6,070,059 in 1966 to 13,794,512 in 1974. Of these enrolled in 1974, over 62 percent were in programs offered in secondary schools. In this period, the funding of vocational programs by the federal government also nearly doubled, from $234 million in 1966 to $413 million in 1974. For fiscal year 1976, this funding rose to $423 million. These financial and enrollment figures reflect only those funds and students involved in the traditional conception of vocational education. They do not include those funds and students involved in the new career education approach to occupational selection.[68]

Distributive Education during the 1960s and 1970s

By the time of the passage of the Vocational Education Act of 1963, distributive education had survived the trials of the 1960s and knew who it could number among its friends. As was previously discussed, the National Retail Dry Goods Association (currently known as the National Retail Merchants Association) was one of the first organizations to come to the aid of distributive education during the crisis of the 1950s. Also numbered among its supporters in that period were the National Retail Furniture Association and the National Hardware Manufacturers' Association. Companies such as W. T. Grant, S. S. Kresge, G. C. Murphy, J. J. Newbury, F. W. Woolworth, and Sears, Roebuck and Company became dedicated proponents of distributive education. Such support from companies and retail associations was well within the tradition of distributive education. From the time of Lucinda Prince, companies that had participated in the training programs or had acquired quality employees from such programs were devoted to the continuation of training programs in retail selling.[69]

The generally good relations between distributive education and small owner-operated stores, large retail chains, and merchant associations have continued to the present. One reason for these good feelings is the willingness of most distributive education teachers and administrators to tailor their programs and time schedules to fit the needs of the merchant and his established working hours. One example of this cooperation was presented at the annual meeting of distributive education teachers and administrators held in Houston, Texas, in December 1976. In one of the workshops, the discussion centered on a project conducted by the Houston Independent School District. The district found that the downtown Houston merchants' greatest need for extra sales help occurred during the lunch period—roughly 11:15 A.M. to 2:00 P.M. The district and its distributive education teachers worked out an arrangement with the participating stores that allowed the students to get to the stores in time to work during the lunch period. This meant an adjustment in the students' class periods. Therefore, in order to assure that the student received the proper amount of classroom time, the stores provided space for classroom instruction. Both the stores and the students appeared to benefit from this arrangement. The stores received their needed help during the short but heavy sales period and the students benefited from having the theory of the classroom so close to the reality of the store.[70]

Enrollment in distributive education programs nearly doubled between 1966 and 1974, from 420,426 to 832,905. Of those enrolled in 1974, 353,339 or slightly more than 42 percent were in secondary programs, 346,352 or slightly less than 42 percent where in adult programs, and 133,214 or nearly 16 percent were in postsecondary programs. Participation in DECA also increased during the 1960s and 1970s. In 1959, DECA reported a membership of just over 19,000. By 1964, the membership had nearly doubled to 36,889. DECA membership numbered 108,226 in 1970 and 166,671 in 1975.[71]

The growth of distributive education programs was also reflected in the increase in the number of educators leading the programs. A federal government report tabulated the number of distributive education teachers in 1970 at 10,458. By 1974 the number had increased by nearly 60 percent to 16,505.[72]

Along with increasing enrollments, distributive education also received an increase in federal funds. In fiscal year 1962, distributive education was allocated $2,565,000 in federal financing. This was increased in fiscal year 1964 to $2,580,000 to $7,046,000 in 1966, and $10,252,942 in fiscal year 1969.[73]

Considering the growing popularity of career education, where does distributive education fit into this popular concept? A number of those in distributive education feel that it can play an important role within career education. Such a belief is not without

justification. *Work in America*, the HEW report that was highly
critical of vocational education, praised the use of cooperative
training in vocational programs. The authors of the report believed cooperative training, when properly used, could be a valuable tool in career education. Such training would allow the student to observe and assist adults in work. It would provide them
with the opportunity to discover what the job was really like and
what problems were inherent in it. Students could learn what they
could and could not do—they would discover some of their personal limitations. Also cooperative training could make school
meaningful to those who found traditional learning situations—in
both vocational and traditional programs—less than stimulating.
And, it would provide an income which could be economically
and emotionally rewarding. These were the advantages that
cooperative training would offer when used as a part of career
education. Distributive education programs, particularly on the
secondary level, are currently offering these advantages and have
for a number of years. Thus, indirectly distributive education
received an accolade from a report that was very critical of
vocational education in general.[74]

The adaptability of the cooperative training part of distributive
education to career education also presented a challenge to those
teaching and administering distributive education progress.
Several writers who commented on this challenge tended to view
it as an opportunity for distributive education. In the grades
before the student becomes eligible to enroll in distributive education, the career education programs would undoubtedly introduce him or her to various careers in all aspects of retailing,
wholesaling, supervision, managerial, and supportive industries.
Thus distributive education had to prepare new programs to offer
the student training in the area of his or her interest. The challenge was to create the programs, establish the classes, and
teach the new courses. If distributive education did not meet this
opportunity, the student would look elsewhere for his or her
training and distributive education would become outmoded if
not obsolete. Also, it was held to be the responsibility of those
in distributive education to oversee the organization of career
education materials relating to distributive occupations and
to supervise how these materials were presented to those in kin-
dergarten through tenth grade. In most cases distributive education, like most other areas of vocational education, was ready
and willing to accept the concept of career education.[75]

Challenges of the Late 1970s and Early 1980s

The mid 1970s saw a rapid expansion of the scope of distributive education. The term *distribution* became the chief designator of a widening field of distributive programs. By the early 1980s, the distribution category not only included distributive education and retail sales but also programs in advertising; apparel and accessories; automotive petroleum; marketing services; finance and credit; food marketing; food service; general retail; hardware building materials; farm and garden; home furniture; industrial materials handling; lodging, reservations, and tourism; small business management; transportation; and warehouse wholesaling.[76]

The total number of students enrolled in vocational education programs grew in 1978 to 19,563,175 of which 63.9 percent were in secondary programs.[77] Distribution programs made up 7.1 percent of all vocational education enrollments with a total of 1,382,044. Of these, 30.6 percent were in the area of general merchandising or retail sales.[78]

The funding of distributive education and vocational education also underwent change in the mid and late 1970s. By 1979 the state and local contribution to vocational programs had more than doubled for the decade to $5,999,090,000 or 90.1 percent of the total funding for vocational education. During the same time, federal contributions to vocational programs grew at a much slower rate and reached $650,120,000 or 9.9 percent of the total funding by 1979.[79] These figures became a focal point of argument in the early 1980s. As inflation cut into the ability of appropriated funds to maintain the past levels of service, those in vocational education called for increased funding from both federal and state/local sources. The election of Ronald Reagan as president of the United States in 1980 brought into power people who looked upon the federal budget as bloated and in need of reduction. The Reagan administration's budgetary reductions were directed at vocational education as well as most other social programs. The general view of the administration toward vocational education was expressed in the report of the National Commission for Employment Policy that was submitted to the president in September 1981. This fourteen-member commission consisted of such persons as Eli Ginzberg, economist and chairman of the commission; Raymond J. Donovan, secretary of labor; Richard S. Schweiker, secretary of health and human services; Terrel H. Bell, secretary of education; Robert P. Nimmo, administrator of the Veterans Administration; J. Clay Smith, acting chairman of the Equal Employment Opportunity Commission; Dwight A. Ink, director of Community Services Administration; Patsy L. Fryman, assistant to the president of the Communications Workers of America; Pedro Garza, national director of SER-Jobs for Progress; Carol S. Gibson, National Urban League; Ruth B. Love, superintendent of schools of Chicago; Leon H. Sullivan, pastor of Zion Baptist Church of Philadelphia; Julius B. Thrower, admissions director of S. D. Bishop State Junior College; and Daniel H. Saks, director of National Commission for Employment Policy. The commission's report on vocational education was titled *The Federal Role in Vocational Education.* It was the position of the commission that the 9.9 percent of total vocational education funding that was contributed by the federal government was a minor amount and of limited value. The commission urged that federal support for vocational education be limited in the future to the establishment and improvement of those programs that were vital to the economy and defense posture of the United States. Only those programs that were in the national interest of the nation should receive federal funding. Federal funding that supported established programs should be eliminated and the entire responsibility for their funding shifted to the states and the local areas. The commission justified its recommendations by citing the rapid increase over the preceding decade in the amount of state and local funds and the corresponding slow increase in federal funds. The rationale was that it would not require much additional effort on the part of the states and local boards to pick up the federal government's 9.9 percent. The commission argued that the rapid local growth would allow the federal government to pull out of the established programs with relatively little impact upon the nature or vitality of the programs.[80]

Those in vocational education did not agree with the recommendations of the commission. The leaders of vocational education viewed the funding figures of the 1970s from a different perspective. In April 1982, Gene Bottoms, executive director of the American Vocational Association, condemned the "New Federalism" of the Reagan administration and its interpretation of the past decade as related to vocational funding. Bottoms stressed that as a result of the increasing popularity of vocational education and its expanding enrollments the per student expenditures had not increased. The increase in total funding had been negated by the increasing number of enrollments. It was Bottoms' contention that the federal support for each student in vocational education had actually declined from $32 per student in 1972 to $15 per student in 1979. He also noted that whereas the state and local contributions had grown rapidly the per student support by such funds which had seen $151 in 1972 was still $151 in 1979. A decrease in the federal involvement would be detrimental to vocational education.[81]

Bottoms was not alone in condemning the "New Federalism" and "Reaganomics." Across the spectrum of vocational education many voiced the same fear that the Reagan administration would cut the heart out of the vocational programs. Some, such as Tony Rodasta, president of the National Association of State Supervisors of Distributive Education, called for the establishment of a grass-roots level organization of students, parents, businessmen, and community people to work for the survival of vocational education. This group of concerned citizens would contact congressmen and other government officials and attempt to educate them about the detrimental impact of proposed budget cuts. This, he hoped, would save vocational education and keep it viable in the 1980s.[82]

Within the little more than two centuries of our nation's existence, vocational education has grown from the few dollars provided by the Ordinance of 1785 to an institution spending billions of dollars annually—federal, state, and local expenditures for vocational education in 1979 exceeded $6.6 billion. However, most of this growth has taken place since the passage of the Smith-Hughes Act in 1917. The growth in enrollment in vocational education is almost as phenomenal as the money expended; from the very few in the beginning to 265,058 in 1920 to 19,563,175 enrolled in programs receiving federal funds in 1979.[83]

Distributive education, or the distributive programs, which in reality are products of this century, demonstrate a similar growth. Enrollment grew from the few students in privately financed store-schools to 1,382,044 students in federally funded programs in 1979.[84]

Whereas vocational education, and distributive education in particular, has had to struggle for existence in the past, and will undoubtedly face funding struggles in the 1980s, they are now an established part of the American educational system. Many changes have been made in their direction, funding, and programs, but both will continue their role in training people to earn a living. Their proponents and opponents must now realize that they are here to stay. The challenge facing vocational education and distributive education in the 1980s will not be one of gaining public acceptance of new programs but will be one of acquiring adequate funding to continue existing programs. Funding in the 1980s may well be vocational education's biggest challenge of the century.

Notes

Chapter 1. Vocational Education before Smith-Hughes

1. Roy W. Robert, *Vocational and Practical Arts Education: History, Development, and Principles*, 3d. ed. (New York: Harper & Row, 1971), p. 24.

2. Ibid., p. 36.

3. Charles Alpheus Bennett, *History of Manual and Industrial Education up to 1870* (Peoria, Ill.: The Manual Arts Press, 1926), pp. 21–22, 24–28; Roberts, *Vocational and Practical Arts Education*, pp. 37–38.

4. Roberts, *Vocational and Practical Arts Education*, pp. 37–38.

5. Bennett, *History of Manual and Industrial Education up to 1870*, p. 267.

6. Layton S. Hawkins, Charles A. Prosser, and John C. Wright, *Development of Vocational Education* (Chicago: American Technical Society, 1951), pp. 6–8; Bennett, *History of Manual and Industrial Education up to 1870*, pp. 268–69.

7. Hawkins et al., *Development of Vocational Education*, pp. 9–11; Bennett, *History of Manual and Industrial Education up to 1870*, pp. 270–72.

8. Bennett, *History of Manual and Industrial Education up to 1870*, pp. 73–74; Erhard F. Wendt, "Brief History of Industrial Arts and Vocational Education," Part 1 *Industrial Arts and Vocational Education* 35, no. 4 (April 1946): 151.

9. S. J. Wanous, "A Chronology of Business Education in the United States," *Business Education Forum* 11, no. 8 Centennial Issue (May 1957): 54.

10. H. G. Good, *A History of American Education*, 2d. ed. (New York: Macmillan, 1962), pp. 73–76; Wanous, "A Chronology of Business Education in the United States," p. 55.

11. Wendt, "Brief History of Industrial Arts and Vocational Education," Part 1, p. 152; Bennett, *History of Manual and Industrial Education up to 1870*.

12. Bennett, *History of Manual and Industrial Education up to 1870*, pp. 325–28.

13. Hawkins, *Development of Vocational Education*, pp. 12–13; Roberts, *Vocational and Practical Arts Education*, pp. 80–81.

14. Bennett, *History of Manual and Industrial Education up to 1870*, pp. 350–52; Good, *A History of American Education*, p. 289.

15. Roberts, *Vocational and Practical Arts Education*, pp. 85–86; Grant Venn, *Man, Education, and Work: Postsecondary Vocational and Technical Education* (Washington, D.C.: American Council on Education, 1964), pp. 42–43.

16. Wendt, "Brief History of Industrial Arts and Vocational Education," Part 1, p. 152; Hawkins, *Development of Vocational Education*, p. 13.

17. Bennett, *History of Manual and Industrial Education up to 1870*, p. 390; Wendt, "Brief History of Industrial Arts and Vocational Education," Part 1, pp. 152–53.

18. Lawrence A. Cremin, *The Transformation of the School: Progressivism in American Education, 1876–1957* (New York: Alfred A. Knopf, 1961), pp. 24–25; Roberts, *Vocational and Practical Arts Education*, pp. 57–58.

135

19. Venn, *Man, Education, and Work*, p. 49; Cremin, *The Transformation of the School*, pp. 25–26.

20. Wendt, "Brief History of Industrial Arts and Vocational Education," Part 1, pp. 153–54; Roberts, *Vocational and Practical Arts Education*, pp. 58–59.

21. Roberts, *Vocational and Practical Arts Education*, pp. 59–60.

22. Bennett, *History of Manual and Industrial Education up to 1870*, pp. 106–120; Melvin L. Barlow, *History of Industrial Education in the United States* (Peoria, Ill.: Charles A. Bennett Company, 1967), pp. 22–23.

23. Bennett, *History of Manual and Industrial Education up to 1870*, pp. 128–35; Barlow, *History of Industrial Education in the United States*, p. 24.

24. Charles Alpheus Bennett, *History of Manual and Industrial Education, 1870 to 1917* (Peoria, Ill.: Charles A. Bennett Company, 1937), pp. 317–18, 336–37; Barlow, *History of Industrial Education in the United States*, pp. 34–35.

25. Bennett, *History of Manual and Industrial Education, 1870 to 1917*, pp. 347–55; Barlow, *History of Industrial Education in the United States*, pp. 35–37; Cremin, *The Transformation of the School*, pp. 27–28.

26. Wilson H. Ivins and William B. Runge, *Work Experience in High School* (New York: Ronald Press, 1951), pp. 44–45; U.S. Department of the Interior, Office of Education, *Cooperative Training in Retail Selling in the Public Schools*, by Glenn Oscar Emick, Vocational Division Bulletin Number 186; Commercial Series No. 10 (Washington, D.C.: U.S. Government Printing Office, 1936 [1937]), p. 5; Bennett, *History of Manual and Industrial Education, 1870 to 1917*, p. 530.

27. U.S. Department of the Interior, *Cooperative Training in Retail Selling in the Public Schools*, p. 5; Bennett, *History of Manual and Industrial Education, 1870 to 1917*, pp. 530–31; Carl T. Brown and William B. Logan, ed., "Fifty Years of Progress in Distributive Education," *American Vocational Journal* 31, no. 9 (December 1956): 59.

28. Bennett, *History of Manual and Industrial Education up to 1870*, pp. 243–46; Merle Curti, *Social Ideas of American Educators: Report of the American Historical Association Commission on the Social Studies*, Part 10 (New York: Charles Scribner's Sons, 1935), p. 289.

29. Curti, *Social Ideas of American Educators*, pp. 288–92; Virgil A. Clift, Archibald W. Anderson, and H. Gordon Hullfish, eds., *Negro Education in America: Its Adequacy, Problems, and Needs*. Sixteenth Yearbook of the John Dewey Society (New York: Harper, 1962), pp. 48–49.

30. Curti, *Social Ideas of American Educators*, pp. 292–99; Clift et al., *Negro Education in America*, pp. 48–51.

31. Erhard F. Wendt, "Brief History of Industrial Arts and Vocational Education," Part II, *Industrial Arts and Vocational Education* 35, no. 5 (May 1946): 203.

32. Venn, *Man, Education, and Work*, pp. 45–46, 48; Roberts, *Vocational and Practical Arts Education*, p. 84.

33. Venn, *Man, Education, and Work*, pp. 46–47; Roberts, *Vocational and Practical Arts Education*, pp. 54–56, 85–86; Bennett, *History of Manual and Industrial Education, 1870 to 1917*, p. 397.

34. Bennett, *History of Manual and Industrial Education, 1870 to 1917*, pp. 362–363; Venn, *Man, Education, and Work*, pp. 48–49; Cremin, *The Transformation of the School*, pp. 30–31.

35. Curti, *Social Ideas of American Educators*, pp. 529–31; Venn, *Man, Education, and Work*, pp. 50–53; Wendt, "Brief History of Industrial Arts and Vocational Education," Part II, p. 203.

36. Wanous, "A Chronology of Business Education in the United States," pp. 54–55.

37. Arthur L. Walker, Harry Huffman, and John A. Beaumont, eds, "Fifty Years of

Progress in Business Education," *American Vocational Journal*. 31, no. 9 (December 1956): 47–48; "Commercial Education," *Cyclopedia of Education*, 1911, II, pp. 143–45; Roberts, *Vocational and Practical Arts Education*, pp. 87–88.

38. "Commercial Education," *Cyclopedia of Education*, pp. 144–47; Walker et al., "Fifty Years of Progress in Business Education," p. 48; Wanous, "A Chronology of Business Education in the United States," pp. 55–56; Roberts, *Vocational and Practical Arts Education*, pp. 87–88.

39. "Commercial Education," *Cyclopedia of Education*, pp. 147–48; Walker, "Fifty Years of Progress in Business Education," p. 48; Wanous, "A Chronology of Business Education in the United States," p. 56.

40. Brown and Logen, "Fifty Years of Progress in Distributive Education," p. 57; Donald K. Beckley, "Early Days in Retail Training," *Business Education World* 29, no. 1 (September 1948) 38; U.S. Department of the Interior,*Cooperative Training in Retail Selling in the Public Schools*, p. 6.

41. Beckley, "Early Days in Retail Training," p. 38.

42. U.S. Department of the Interior, Office of Education, *Cooperative Part-Time Retail Training Programs*; *Supervision, Coordination, and Teaching*, by Kenneth B. Haas, Vocational Division Bulletin no. 205; Business Education Series Number 12 (Washington, D.C.: U.S. Government Printing Office, 1939), pp. 1–2; U.S. Department of the Interior, *Cooperative Training in Retail Selling in the Public Schools*, p. 6; Ruth Sawyer, "Have You Met Mrs. Prince?" *Good Housekeeping*, 72 (January 1921): 118; Lucinda W. Prince, "Training for Efficiency in the Department Store," *Bookman*, 43 (April 1916): 190.

43. U.S. Department of the Interior, *Cooperative Part-Time Retail Training Programs*, pp. 2–3; Prince, "Training for Efficiency in the Department Store," p. 190; Beckley, "Early Days in Retail Training," p. 40.

44. U.S. Department of the Interior, *Cooperative Part-Time Retail Training* Programs, pp. 2–3; Beckley, "Early Days in Retail Training," p. 40.

45. Sawyer, "Have You Met Mrs. Prince?", p. 119.

46. Ivins and Runge, *Work Experience in High School*, p. 44; U.S. Department of the Interior, *Cooperative Training in Retail Selling in the Public Schools*, pp. 6–8; Beckley, "Early Days in Retail Training," p. 40; U.S. Department of the Interior, *Cooperative Part-Time Retail Training Programs*, p. 4.

47. Frederick G. Nichols, "The Background of Distributive Education," *National Business Education Quarterly* 11, no. 2 (March 1943): 11; Ivins and Runge, *Work Experience in High School*, p. 46; Hawkins, *Development of Vocational Education*, p. 153.

48. Ivins and Runge, *Work Experience in High School*, p. 46; Nichols, "The Background of Distributive Education," p. 9.

49. Ivins and Runge, *Work Experience in High School*, pp. 58–63; U.S. Department of the Interior, *Cooperative Training in Retail Selling in the Public Schools*, pp. 7–8; U.S. Department of the Interior, *Cooperative Part-Time Retail Training Programs*, pp. 4–5; Nichols, "The Background of Distributive Education," pp. 10–11.

50. Hawkins et al., *Development of Vocational Education*, pp. 32–33; Bennett, *History of Manual and Industrial Education, 1870 to 1917*, pp. 513–14; U.S. Department of the Interior, Office of Education, *Federal Cooperation in Agricultural Extension Work, Vocational Education, and Vocational Rehabilitation*, by Lloyd E. Blauch, Bulletin no. 15 (1933) (Washington, D.C.: U.S. Government Printing Office, 1935, reprinted by Arno Press and New York Times, 1969), pp. 22–23.

51. Hawkins et al.,*Development of Vocational Education*, p. 33; Bennett, *History of Manual and Industrial Education, 1870 to 1917*, p. 514.

52. Bennett, *History of Manual and Industrial Education, 1870 to 1917*, pp. 514–15; Hawkins, et al., *Development of Vocational Education*, pp. 34–36.

53. Bennett, *History of Manual and Industrial Education, 1870 to 1917*, pp. 515–17; Hawkins et al., *Development of Vocational Education*, pp. 35–37; Roberts, *Vocational and Practical Arts Education*, pp. 97–100.

54. Roberts, *Vocational and Practical Arts Education*, pp. 99–100; Hawkins, *Development of Vocational Education*, p. 40.

55. Roberts, *Vocational and Practical Arts Education*, pp. 99; Hawkins et al., *Development of Vocational Education*, pp. 40–41, 44.

56. Hawkins et al., *Development of Vocational Education*, p. 49.

57. Hawkins et al., *Development of Vocational Education*, pp. 38–50; Roberts, *Vocational and Practical Arts Education*, pp. 96–102; U.S. Department of the Interior, *Federal Cooperation*, pp. 22–28.

58. Bennett, *History of Manual and Industrial Education, 1870 to 1917*, pp. 540–41.

59. Ibid., p. 541.

60. Ibid., pp. 541–42.

Chapter 2. The Smith-Hughes Act

1. Hsien Lu, *Federal Role in Education; A Comprehensive Study of Federal Relations to Education in the United States—Their Past, Present, and Future* (New York: American Press, 1968), pp. 29–30; Richard G. Axt, *The Federal Government and Financing Higher Education* (New York: Columbia University Press, 1952), pp. 22–24; Dennis E. Roley, "The Prospects Are Bright," *Business Education Forum* 22, no. 8 (May 1968): 7.

2. Axt, *The Federal Government and Financing Higher Education*, pp. 25–27; Lu, *Federal Role in Education*, p. 30.

3. Axt, *The Federal Government and Financing Higher Education*, pp. 24–28.

4. William T. Bawden, "Some Leaders in Industrial Education," Part I, *Industrial Arts and Vocational Education* 40, no. 2 (February 1951): 53.

5. Good, *A History of American Education*, pp. 291–93; Isaac Leon Kandel, *Federal Aid for Vocational Education, A Report to the Carnegie Foundation for the Advancement of Teaching*, Bulletin no. 10, 1917 (New York: Carnegie Foundation for the Advancement of Teaching, 1917), pp. 3–15; Bawden, "Some Leaders in Industrial Education," Part I, p. 53; Lynn E. Stockwell, "Federal Aid to Vocational Education," *Industrial Education Magazine* 28, no. 6. (December 1926): 179.

6. Axt, *The Federal Government and Financing Higher Education*, pp. 40–43; Bawden, "Some Leaders in Industrial Education," Part I, pp. 53–54; Good, *A History of American Education*, pp. 293–95; Kandel, *Federal Aid for Vocational Education*, pp. 16–19; *Land Grant Colleges Act* (First Morrill Act), *U.S. Code*, vol. 1, secs. 301, 304 (1970).

7. Axt, *The Federal Government and Financing Higher Education*, pp. 52–59; Lu, *Federal Role in Education*, pp. 45–49; Good, *A History of American Education*, pp. 299–300; U.S. Department of the Interior, *Federal Cooperation*, p. 40; *Agricultural Colleges Act of 1890* (Second Morrill Act), *U.S. Code*, vol. 1, secs. 321–26, 328 (1970).

8. U.S. Department of the Interior, *Federal Cooperation*, pp. 49–51; Stockwell, "Federal Aid to Vocational Education," p. 179; *Amendment to the Agricultural Colleges Act of 1890* (Nelson Amendment), *U.S. Code*, Vol. 1, sec. 322 (1970).

9. Lu, *Federal Role in Education*, pp. 129–130; W. John Copper, "Office of Education," *Scientific Monthly* 36, no. 2 (February 1933): 121–23.

10. Lu, *Federal Role in Education*, pp. 130; U.S. Department of the Interior, *Federal Cooperation*, p. 39; Cooper, "Office of Education," p. 123.

11. Barlow, *History of Industrial Education in the United States*, p. 134; U.S. Department of the Interior, *Federal Cooperation*, p. 39; Lu, *Federal Role in Education*, pp. 131–32; Cooper, "Office of Education," pp. 123–25.

12. Axt, *The Federal Government and Financing Higher Education*, pp. 50–51; Bawden, "Some Leaders in Industrial Education," Part 1, p. 54.

13. Axt, *The Federal Government and Financing Higher Education*, pp. 51–52; Lu, *Federal Role in Education*, pp. 50–51; *Hatch Act, U.S. Code*, Vol. 1, secs. 361(1)–361(i) (1970).

14. U.S. Department of the Interior, *Federal Cooperation*, p. 41; Bawden, "Some Leaders in Industrial Education," Part I, p. 54; *Agriculture Experiment Stations* (Adams Act), *U.S. Code*, Vol. 1, sec. 369 (1958).

15. U.S. Department of the Interior, *Federal Cooperation*, p. 41.

16. Ibid., pp. 41–43.

17. Axt, *The Federal Government and Financing Higher Education*, pp. 62–63; U.S. Department of the Interior, *Federal Cooperation*, pp. 38–39, 44–45.

18. Hawkins et al., *Development of Vocational Education*, pp. 62–63; Roberts, *Vocational and Practical Arts Education*, pp. 92–93; Barlow, *History of Industrial Education in the United States*, p. 52; Bennett, *History of Manual and Industrial Education, 1870 to 1917*, pp. 517–18.

19. Barlow, *History of Industrial Education in the United States*, p. 55; U.S. Department of the Interior, *Federal Cooperation*, p. 19; Cremin, *The Transformation of the School*, pp. 52–53.

20. U.S. Department of the Interior, *Federal Cooperation*, pp. 19–20; Arthur G. Wirth, "Charles A. Prosser and the Smith-Hughes Act," *Educational Forum* 36, no. 3 (March 1972): 365–67.

21. Hawkins et al., *Development of Vocational Education*, pp. 73–74; Barlow, *History of Industrial Education in the United States*, pp. 75–81.

22. Cremin, *The Transformation of the School*, pp. 41–50; Roberts, *Vocational and Practical Arts Education*, pp. 91–92.

23. U.S. Department of the Interior, *Federal Cooperation*, pp. 17–18; Roberts, *Vocational and Practical Arts Education*, p. 94; Barlow, *History of Industrial Education in the United States*, pp. 81–83.

24. U.S. Department of the Interior, *Federal Cooperation*, p. 16; Philip R. V. Curoe, *Educational Attitudes and Policies of Organized Labor in the United States* (New York: Teachers College, Columbia University, 1926), p. 162.

25. Curoe, *Educational Attitudes and Policies of Organized Labor*, pp. 127, 134–36, 162–65; U.S. Department of the Interior, *Federal Cooperation*, pp. 16–17; Hawkins et al., *Development of Vocational Education*, pp. 53–54, 415–18.

26. Curoe, *Educational Attitudes and Policies of Organized Labor*, p. 136; Barlow, *History of Industrial Education in the United States*, p. 379; U.S. Department of the Interior, *Federal Cooperation*, p. 15; Hawkins et al., *Development of Vocational Education*, pp. 51–52, 420–21.

27. Hawkins et al., *Development of Vocational Education*, pp. 421–22; Roberts, *Vocational and Practical Arts Education*, pp. 95–96.

28. U.S. Department of the Interior, *Federal Cooperation*, p. 55; Hawkins et al., *Development of Vocational Education*, pp. 66–70.

29. U.S. Department of the Interior, *Federal Cooperation*, pp. 47–51; Roberts, *Vocational and Practical Arts Education*, p. 104.

30. U.S. Department of the Interior, *Federal Cooperation*, pp. 52–53.

31. U.S. Department of the Interior, *Federal Cooperation*, pp. 53–54; Bennett, *History of Manual and Industrial Education, 1870 to 1917*, p. 543; William T. Bawden, "Some Leaders in Industrial Education," Part II, *Industrial Arts and Vocational Education* 46, no. 4 (April 1951): 147.

32. U.S. Department of the Interior, *Federal Cooperation*, pp. 55–60; Barlow, *History of Industrial Education in the United States*, pp. 55–56; Bennett, *History of Manual and

Industrial Education, 1870 to 1917, pp. 543–44.

33. U.S. Department of the Interior, *Federal Cooperation*, pp. 61–67; Barlow, *History of Industrial Education in the United States*, pp. 57–58; Bawden, "Some Leaders in Industrial Education," Part II, p. 147.

34. Roberts, *Vocational and Practical Arts Education*, p. 105; Bennett, *History of Manual and Industrial Education, 1870 to 1917*, p. 545; U.S. Department of the Interior, *Federal Cooperation*, p. 72.

35. U.S. Department of the Interior, *Federal Cooperation*, pp. 67–84; Barlow, *History of Industrial Education in the United States*, p. 58; Bennett, *History of Manual and Industrial Education, 1870 to 1917*, pp. 545–46.

36. U.S. Department of the Interior, *Federal Cooperation*, pp. 67–94; Bawden, "Some Leaders in Industrial Education," Part I, p. 54.

37. Venn, *Man, Education, and Work*, pp. 56–57; Hawkins et al., *Development of Vocational Education*, pp. 80–81.

38. Bawden, "Some Leaders in Industrial Education," Part II, p. 147; Hawkins et al., *Development of Vocational Education*, pp. 81, 543; U.S. Department of the Interior, *Federal Cooperation*, p. 97; "The Federal Plan for Vocational Education," *Survey* 35, no. 24, March 11, 1916, p. 692.

39. U.S. Department of the Interior, *Federal Cooperation*, p. 98; Hawkins et al., *Development of Vocational Education*, pp. 82, 543–44; Venn, *Man, Education, and Work*, p. 58; "The Federal Plan for Vocational Education," p. 692.

40. Bennett, *History of Manual and Industrial Education, 1870 to 1917*, pp. 546–47; U.S. Department of the Interior, *Federal Cooperation*, p. 98.

41. Hawkins et al., *Development of Vocational Education*, pp. 82, 547–49; U.S. Department of the Interior, *Federal Cooperation*, pp. 99–100.

42. Bawden, "Some Leaders in Industrial Education," Part II, p. 148; Hoke Smith *Biographical Dictionary of the American Congress, 1774–1949* (Washington, D.C.: Government Printing Office, 1950), pp. 1827–28.

43. Bawden, "Some Leaders in Industrial Education," Part II, p. 149; Dudley Mayes Huges *Biographical Dictionary of the American Congress, 1774–1927* (Washington, D.C.: U.S. Government Printing Office, 1928), p. 1126.

44. U.S. Department of the Interior, *Federal Cooperation*, pp. 100–101; Hawkins et al., *Development of Vocational Education*, pp. 82–85, 90; Wirth, "Charles A. Prosser and the Smith-Hughes Act," pp. 366–67.

45. U.S. Department of the Interior, *Federal Cooperation*, pp. 102–5; Hawkins et al., *Development of Vocational Education*, pp. 86–87.

46. U.S. Department of the Interior, *Federal Cooperation*, pp. 102–4; Hawkins et al., *Development of Vocational Education*, pp. 421–22.

47. U.S. Department of the Interior, *Federal Cooperation*, pp. 105–8; Hawkins et al., *Development of Vocational Education*, pp. 88–89, 118.

48. U.S. Department of the Interior, Office of Education, Advisory Committee on Education, *Vocational Education*, by John Dale Russell and associates, Staff Study no. 8 (Washington, D.C.: U.S. Government Printing Office, 1938), pp. 16–17; "The Smith-Hughes Act," *Industrial Arts Magazine* 6, no. 4 (April 1917): 168; C. M. Arthur, "Vocational Education," *Congressional Digest* 13, no. 8–9 (August–September 1934): 199; *Vocational Education Act of 1917* (Smith-Hughes Act), *Statutes at Large* 40 (1917).

49. Arthur, "Vocational Education," pp. 199–200; "The Smith-Hughes Act," *Industrial Arts Magazine*, pp. 168–69; *Vocational Educational Act of 1917* (Smith-Hughes Act), *Statutes at Large*, 40 (1917).

50. "The Smith-Hughes Act," *Industrial Arts Magazine*, p. 168; Arthur, "Vocational Education," p. 200; *Vocational Education Act of 1917* (Smith-Hughes Act), *Statutes at Large* 40 (1917).

51. William T. Bawden, "The Federal Board for Vocational Education," *Manual Training Magazine* 19, no. 1 (September 1917): 1, 4; U.S. Department of the Interior, *Federal Cooperation*, pp. 214–15; Hawkins, *Development of Vocational Education*, pp. 136, 142–46.

52. "The Administration of the Smith-Hughes Act," *School and Society*, 6, no. 151, November 17, 1917, p. 594; U.S. Department of the Interior, *Vocational Education*, pp. 36–37; Hawkins, *Development of Vocational Education*, pp. 165–68.

53. Hawkins et al., *Development of Vocational Education*, p. 167; Barlow, *History of Industrial Education in the United States*, p. 118.

54. U.S. Department of the Interior, *Vocational Education*, p. 38; Barlow, *History of Industrial Education in the United States*, p. 118.

55. Bawden, "Some Leaders in Industrial Education," Part II, p. 149.

56. *Vocational Education Act of 1917* (Smith-Hughes Act), *Statutes at Large*, 40, Sec. 6 (1917).

57. "A Brief History of the U.S. Office of Education," *Business Education World*, 26, no. 7 (March 1946): 396; Nichols, "The Background of Distributive Education," pp. 11; Hawkins et al., *Development of Vocational Education*, p. 225.

58. Ivins and Runge, *Work Experience in High School*, pp. 43–44; Nichols, "The Background of Distributive Education," pp. 11, 48; Walker, "Fifty Years of Progress in Business Education," p. 49.

59. Walker et al., "Fifty Years of Progress in Business Education," p. 49; Nichols, "The Background of Distributive Education," pp. 9–10, 12, 50; Brown, "Fifty Years of Progress in Distributive Education," p. 57; Roberts, *Vocational and Practical Arts Education*, pp. 201–2.

Chapter 3. Vocational Education in the 1920s and 1930s

1. U.S. Department of the Interior, *Vocational Education*, pp. 69–71; U.S. Department of the Interior, *Federal Cooperation*, p. 217; Hawkins, et al., *Development of Vocational Education*, p. 181.

2. U.S. Department of the Interior, *Vocational Education*, p. 35; Hawkins et al., *Development of Vocational Education*, p. 203; *Vocational Education Act of 1917* (Smith-Hughes Act), *Statutes at Large* 29, sec. 8, (1917).

3. Hawkins et al., *Development of Vocational Education*, pp. 203–5.

4. Roberts, *Vocational and Practical Arts Education*, p. 149; Hawkins, *Development of Vocational Education*, p. 361; "The Federal Subsidy to Vocational Education," *Industrial Arts Magazine* 15, no. 3 (March 1926): 101–2.

5. Clarence D. Lehman, "How the Smith-Hughes Act Affects Vocational Expenditure," *Nation's Schools* 7, no. 5 (May 1931): 42–43.

6. "The Forward March in Vocational Education," *School Life* 21, no. 6 (February 1936): 152–53; U.S. Department of the Interior, *Federal Cooperation*, pp. 230–31; Hawkins, *Development of Vocational Education*, pp. 352–53.

7. Hawkins et al., *Development of Vocational Education*, p. 356.

8. U.S. Department of the Interior, *Federal Cooperation*, p. 219.

9. Hawkins et al., *Development of Vocational Education*, pp. 430–41.

10. U.S. Department of the Interior, *Federal Cooperation*, pp. 164–66; Hawkins, *Development of Vocational Education*, pp. 442–44, 446; *Vocational Rehabilitation Act* (Smith-Sears Act), *Statutes at Large* 40 (1918).

11. U.S. Department of the Interior, *Federal Cooperation*, pp. 165–72; Hawkins et al., *Development of Vocational Education*, pp. 455, 459–67; *Vocational Rehabilitation Act* (Smith-Fess Act), *Statutes at Large* 10 (1920).

12. Charles Franklin Bauder, "Vocational Education and the New Deal," *Industrial Education Magazine* 37, no. 3 (May 1935): 135; "The Forward March in Vocational Education," *School Life*, p. 152.

13. U.S. Department of the Interior, Office of Education, Advisory Committee on Education, *Special Programs of Negro Education*, by Doxey Alphonso Wilkerson, Staff Study no. 12 (Washington, D.C.: U.S. Government Printing Office, 1939), pp. 77–79, 81, 96–99; U.S. Department of the Interior, Office of Education, *Vocational Education and Guidance of Negroes*, by Ambrose Caliver, Bulletin no. 38 (Washington, D.C.: U.S. Government Printing Office, 1937), p. 31.

14. U.S. Department of the Interior, *Federal Cooperation*, pp. 235.

15. Ibid., pp. 237–39.

16. Ibid., pp. 240–42.

17. Hawkins et al., *Development of Vocational Education*, pp. 224–226.

18. Nichols, "The Background of Distributive Education," pp. 10–11, 44.

19. Ibid., pp. 12, 48–50.

20. Ibid., pp. 12, 44, 48–50.

21. Ibid., pp. 12, 44–45; U.S. Department of the Interior, *Cooperative Training in Retail Selling in the Public Schools*, p. 190.

22. Nichols, "The Background of Distributive Education," p. 46; U.S. Department of the Interior, *Cooperative Training in Retail Selling in the Public Schools*, pp. 191–92.

23. Rae C. Williams, "Thirty-two Years in D. E., *Business Education World*, 33, no. 5 (January 1953): 238; Jeanie Cross, "Simulated Stores Stimulate Learning: Many Examples presented at Anaheim," *American Vocational Journal* 51, 2 (February 1976): 45–47.

24. Barlow, *History of Industrial Education in the United States*, pp. 127–31; U.S. Department of the Interior, *Vocational Education*, p. 28.

25. Hawkins et al., *Development of Vocational Education*, pp. 157–59; U.S. Department of the Interior, *Federal Cooperation*, pp. 151–52; U.S. Department of the Interior, *Vocational Education*, pp. 28–29.

26. U.S. Department of the Interior, *Federal Cooperation*, p. 141; Hawkins et al., *Development of Vocational Education*, p. 406.

27. U.S. Department of the Interior, *Federal Cooperation*, pp. 141–43; U.S. Department of the Interior, *Vocational Education*, pp. 18–19; *Act to Provide for Further Development of Vocational Education in the Several States and Territories* (George-Reed Act), *Statutes at Large* 45, 1151 (1929).

28. U.S. Department of the Interior, *Federal Cooperation*, pp. 154–59, 162.

29. Ibid., p. 161; U.S. Department of the Interior, *Vocational Education*, p. 19, *Act to Provide for Further Development of Vocational Education in the Several States and Territories* (George-Ellzey Act), *Statues at Large*, 48 (1934).

30. Walter Franklin George, *Current Biography, 1943* (New York: H. H. Wilson, 1944), pp. 229–30; Walter Franklin George, *Biographical Dictionary of the American Congress, 1774–1949* (Washington, D.C.: U.S. Government Printing Office, 1950), p. 1203; U.S. Department of the Interior, *Vocational Education*, pp. 19–20.

31. U.S. Department of the Interior, *Vocational Education*, pp. 19–20.

32. Ibid., pp. 20–21; U.S. Congress, House, Debate on H.R. 12120, 74th Cong., 2nd sess., May 26, 1936, *Congressional Record*, 80, 7956, 7960; U.S. Congress, Senate, Letter from L. J. Taber, Master, National Grange supporting S. 2883 on Vocational Education, 74th Cong., 2nd sess., February 18, 1936, *Congressional Record*, 2279.

33. U.S. Congress, Senate, Debate on Amendments to S. 2883, 74th Cong., 2nd Sess., April 28, 1936, *Congressional Record* 80, 6268–29; U.S. Congress, House, Debate on H.R. 12120, 74th Cong., 2nd sess., May 26, 1936, *Congressional Record* 7955–60, 7965.

34. U.S. Department of the Interior, *Vocational Education*, pp. 21–23; U.S. Congress, House, Debate on H.R. 6958, Amendments to Department of the Interior Appropria-

tions Bill, 1938, 75th Cong., 1st sess., May 20, 1937, *Congressional Record* 81, 4849–61; U.S. Congress, Senate, Joint Resolution of the Legislature of the State of Wisconsin Urging the Congress of the United States to Allocate to the States the Whole Appropriations Authorized by the George-Deen Act for Vocational Education, 75th Cong., 1st sess., February 23, 1937, *Congressional Record* 81, 1467; *Act to Provide for the Further Development of Vocational Education in the Several States and Territories* (George-Deen Act), *Statutes at Large* 49 (1936); U.S. Congress, Senate, Debate on H.R. 6958, Department of the Interior Appropriations, 75th Cong., 1st sess., June 28, 1937, *Congressional Record* 81, 6396–6406.

35. U.S. Department of the Interior, *Vocational Education*, p. 21; Brown, "Fifty Years of Progress in Distributive Education," p. 58; *Act to Provide for the Further Development of Vocational Education in the Several States and Territories* (George-Deen Act), *Statutes at Large* 49, (1936).

36. Charles M. Arthur, "George-Deen Act and Its Implication," *School Life* 22, no. 5 (January 1937): 133; U.S. Congress, Senate, Debate on Amendments to S. 2883, 74th Cong., 2nd sess., April 28, 1936, *Congressional Record* 80, 6268; *Act to Provide for the Further Development of Vocational Education in the Several States and Territories* (George-Deen Act), *Statutes at Large*, 41 (1936).

37. U.S. Department of the Interior, Office of Education, *Statement of for the Administration of Policies of Vocational Education*, Vocational Education Bulletin no 1 (Revised February 1937. Washington, D.C.: Government Printing Office, 1937), p. 66–67.

38. Ibid., p. 67.

39. U.S. Department of the Interior, Office of Education, *Distributive Education, Organization and Administration*, by Kenneth B. Hass, Vocational Division Bulletin Number 211, business Education Series Number 13 (Washington, D.C.: U.S. Government Printing Office, 1940), pp. 2, 5–6; Frederick G. Nichols, "Vocational Training for the Distributive Occupations Under the George-Deen Act," *Education Digest* 3, no. 5 (January 1938): 4–5; *Act to Provide for Further Development of Vocational Education in the Several States and Territories* (George-Deen Act), *Statutes at Large*, 4, sec. 6, (1936).

40. B. Frank Kyker, "Five Years of Distributive Education Under the George-Deen Act," *National Business Education Quarterly* 11, no. 3 (March 1943): 13; Nichols, "Vocational Training for the Distributive Occupations Under the George-Deen Act," pp. 4–5; Earl B. Webb, "Distributive Occupations Education Under the George-Deen Act," Chapter 19 of *Improvement of Classroom Teaching in Business Education*, Twelfth Yearbook of the Eastern Commercial Teachers' Association (Philadelphia: Eastern Commercial Teachers Association, 1939), pp. 146–49; Frederick G. Nichols. "Business Education—Clerical and Distributive." *National Society for Study of Education*, Forty-second Year-book, Part I (Chicago: University of Chicago Press, 1943), pp. 220–21.

41. "A Criticism of the George-Deen Vocational Education Act," *Elementary School Journal* 37, no. 7 (March 1937): 488–90.

Chapter 4. The War Years and After

1. U.S. Department of the Interior, *Vocational Education*, pp. iii, 1–2; "President Roosevelt's Message on the Congressional Appropriation for Vocational Education," *School and Society* 46, no. 1182, August 21, 1937, pp. 249–251.

2. U.S. Department of the Interior, *Vocational Education*, pp. 126–236, 233–40.

3. David Snedden, "Vocational Education: Next Stages," *School and Society* 46, no. 1200, December 25, 1937, pp. 813–18; David Snedden, "Vocational Education: Another Milestone?" *School and Society* 49, no, 1275, June 3, 1939, pp. 685–91.

4. U.S. Department of the Interior, Office of Education, *Vocational Education in the Years Ahead: A Report of a Committee to Study Postwar Problems in Vocational Education*, Vocational Division Bulletin No. 234; General Series No. 7 (Washington, D.C.: U.S. Government Printing Office, 1945), pp. 254–57.

5. Ibid., pp. 11–12.

6. Ibid., pp. 31–35, 35, 43–49.

7. U.S. Department of the Interior, *Vocational Education*, pp. 248–59, 284–89. The entire Broach and Parker study appears as Appendix A of *Vocational Education*.

8. U.S. Department of the Interior, *Vocational Education in the Years Ahead*, pp. 161–62.

9. John A. Beaumont, "The Federal Role in Distributive Education," *American Vocational Journal* 38, no. 9 (December 1963): 37; "Wartime Distibutive Education," *Education for Victory* 1, no. 11, August 1, 1942, p. 19.

10. U.S. Department of the Interior, *Vocational Education in the Years Ahead*, pp. 163–64; "Progress of Vocational Education Programs: States Overmatch Federal Grants," *Education for Victory* 1, no. 32, June 15, 1943, pp. 24–25; "Wartime Distributive Education," *Education for Victory*, p. 19.

11. U.S. Department of the Interior, *Vocational Education in the Years Ahead*, p. 164.

12. Ibid., pp. 164–65.

13. Ibid., pp. 11–13.

14. Hawkins et al., *Development of Vocational Education*, pp. 476–78; *Second Deficiency Appropriations Act, 1940, Statutes at Large* 54 (1940); *First Supplemental Civil Functions Appropriations Act, 1941, Statutes at Large* 54 (1940).

15. Hawkins, *Development of Vocational Education*, pp. 489–501.

16. Buel W. Patch, "Full Employment," *Editorial Research Reports* 2, no. 4, July 30, 1945, pp. 65, 73–74; Arthur F. McClure, *The Truman Administration and the Problems of Post-War Labor, 1945–1948* (Rutherford, N.J.: Fairleigh Dickinson University Press, 1968), p. 185.

17. Patch, "Full Employment," pp. 62–63; McClure, *The Truman Administration*, pp. 186–87.

18. Patch, "Full Employment," pp. 74–75; McClure, *The Truman Administration*, pp. 192–93.

19. McClure, *The Truman Administration*, pp. 194–200; *Employment Act of 1946, Statutes at Large* 60 (1946).

20. McClure, *The Truman Administration*, pp. 193–94; Patch, "Full Employment," pp. 76–78.

21. Leon Isaac Kandel, *The Impact of the War Upon American Education* (Chapell Hill: University of North Carolina Press, 1948), pp. 66–67, 70–71.

22. *American Education in the Postwar Period*, Part I, *Curriculum Reconstruction*, edited by Nelson B. Henry, Forty-fourth yearbook, National Society for the Study of Education (Chicago: University of Chicago Press, 1945), pp. 30–31; Cremin, *The Transformation of the School*, p. 338.

23. Kandel, *The Impact of the War Upon American Education*, pp. 67–69, 73; U.S. President, *Public Papers of the Presidents of the United States: Harry S. Truman, 1946* (Washington, D.C.: U.S. Government Printing Office, 1962), p. 65.

24. John C. Wright, "Vocational Education and the National Welfare," *Education* 66, no. 4 (December 1945): 205; Venn, *Man, Education, and Work*, p. 61; U.S. Department of the Interior, *Vocational Education in the Years Ahead*, pp. 11–12; M. D. Mobley, "Vocational Education and Full Employment," *Education* 66, no. 4 (December 1945): 199–200.

25. Cecil Winfield Scott and Clyde M. Hill, eds., *Public Education Under Criticism* (New York: Prentice-Hall, 1954), pp. 55–58.

26. Alonzo G. Grace, "Vocational Education and the Post-War Period," *Education* 66, no. 4 (December 1945): 230–32.

27. Venn, *Man, Education, and Work*, p. 61; Grace, "Vocational Education and the Post-War Period," pp. 229–230; Mobley, "Vocational Education and Full Employment," p. 197; U.S. Department of the Interior, Office of Education, *Vocational Training Problems When the War Ends*, by John C. Wright, Vocational Division Leaflet No. 12 (Washington, D.C.: U.S. Government Printing Office, 1943), p. 4.

28. Hawkins et al., *Development of Vocational Education*, p. 409.

29. Herbert A. Tonne, "Senate Vocational Education Bill Hearings," *Journal of Business Education* 21, no. 1 (September 1945): 34; "Testimony on the Vocational Education Bill," *Journal of Business Education* 21, no. 2 (October 1945): 28–29.

30. "Testimony on the Vocational Education Bill," *Journal of Business Education* 21, no. 6 (January 1946): 29.

31. "Statement of Dr. Paul H. Nystrom at the Hearings for the Vocational Education Bill," *Journal of Business Education* 21, no. 3 (November, 1945): pp. 26–27; "Testimony of the Vocational Education Bill," *Journal of Business Education* 21, no. 4 (January 1946): 29.

32. "Bill to Provide Additional Federal Aid for Vocational Education," *Higher Education*, 1, no. 10, May 15, 1945, p. 6; "The Barden Vocational Education Bill," *Journal of Business Education* 21, no. 4 (December 1945): 26; Tonne, "Senate Vocational Education Bill Hearings," p. 34; "Testimony on the Vocational Education Bill," *Journal of Business Education*, 21, no. 2 (October 1945): 28–29.

33. "Bill to Provide Additional Federal Aid for Vocational Education," *Higher Education*, p. 6; Tonne, "Senate Vocational Education Bill Hearings," p. 34; "Testimony on the Vocational Education Bill," *Journal of Business Education* 21, no. 4 (October 1945): 28–29; "The Barden Vocational Education Bill," *Journal of Business Education*, p. 26; Arthur B. Moehlman, "Vocational Bills Threaten Balance and Unity of Secondary Education," *Nation's Schools* 34, no. 5 (November 1944): 19.

34. "The Barden Vocational Education Bill," *Journal of Business Education*, p. 26; "Testimony on the Vocational Education Bill," *Journal of Business Education* (October 1945): 28–29; Moehlman, "Vocational Bills Threaten Balance and Unity of Secondary Education," p. 19.

35. L. H. Dennis, "The New George-Barden Vocational Education Act," *Industrial Arts and Vocational Education* 35, no. 9 (November 1946): 18A *Vocational Education Act of 1946* (George-Barden Act), *Statutes at Large* 40 (1946).

Chapter 5. Years of Triumphs and Trials

1. *The DECA Handbook*, 1975 Rev. ed. (Washington, D.C.: The Distributive Education Clubs of America, 1975), p. 15; Irl S. Newham, "The Historical Development of the Distributive Education Clubs of America" (Master's thesis, Central Missouri State University, 1966), p. 18.

2. *The DECA Handbook*, p. 15.

3. Ibid., p. 16.

4. "A. V. A. Defends Earmarked Funds," *Nation's Schools*, 43, no. 1 (January 1949): 50.

5. "D. E. Future Exploding in Congress," *Business Education World* 31, no. 10 (June 1951): 489; "Increased Federal Aid of D. E. Seems Likely," *Journal of Business Education* 28, no. 8 (May 1953): 348.

6. "Increased Federal Aid of D. E. Seems Likely," *Journal of Business Education*, p. 348; Herbert A. Tonne, "Three Cheers for McCargo!" *Journal of Business Education*

28, no. 7 (April 1953): 287; Roberts, *Vocational and Practical Arts Education*, p. 454.

7. "Increased Federal Aid of D. E. Seems Likely," *Journal of Business Education*, p. 348; Tonne, "Three Cheers for McCargo!" pp. 280–87; *Departments of Labor, and Health, Education, and Welfare, and Related Agencies Appropriations Act, 1954, Statutes at Large*, 67, Title II, 250 (1953); *Departments of Labor, and Health, Education, and Welfare, and Related Agencies Appropriations Act, 1955, Statutes at Large*, 68, Title II, 439 (1954); *Departments of Labor, and Health, Education, and Welfare, and Related Agencies Appropriations Act, 1956, Statutes* at Large, 69, Title II, 402 (1955).

8. Elaine Exton, "The Federal Security Agency Attains Cabinet Rank," *School Board Journal* (May 1953): 45; "Increased Federal Aid of D. E. Seems Likely," *Journal of Business Education*, p. 348.

9. *Federal Role in Education* (Washington, D.C.: Congressional Quarterly Service, 1965), p. 11; U. S., Department of Health, Education, and Welfare, Office of Education, *Education for a Changing World of Work, Report of the Panel of Consultants on Vocational Education* (Washington, D.C.: U.S. Government Printing Office, 1963), pp. 24–25; *Act to Promote the Fishing Industry in the United States and Its Territories by Providing for the Training of Needed Personnel for Such Industry, Statutes at Large* 70, (1956); Health Amendments Act of 1956, *Statutes at Large* 70, Title III, 925–29 (1956).

10. Federal Role in Education, pp. 8–9; Venn, *Man, Education, and Work*, p. 114; *National Defense Education Act of 1958, Statutes at Large* 62, Title VIII, sec. 301–7, 1598–1601 (1958).

11. Elaine Exton, "A Progress Report on Vocational Education," *Industrial Arts and Vocational Education* 49, no. 1 (January 1960): 18–19; *Federal Role in Education*, pp. 8, 11; U.S. Department of Health, Education, and Welfare, *Education for a Changing World of Work*, p. 25; *National Defense Education Act of 1958, Statutes at Large*, 62 (1958).

12. U.S. Department of Health, Education, and Welfare, *Education for a Changing World of Work*, p. 14.

13. Venn, *Man, Education, and Work*, pp. 4–5; U. S., Department of Health, Education, and Welfare, *Education for a Changing World of Work*, pp. 14–15.

14. Roy Dugger, "The Vocational Act of 1963," *National Association of Secondary School Principals, Bulletin* 49, no. 301 (May 1965): 17–18; U. S., Department of Health, Education, and Welfare, *Education for a Changing World of Work*, pp. 14–15.

15. U.S. Department of Health, Education, and Welfare, Office of Education, *National Advisory Council on Vocational Education, Vocational Education: The Bridge Between Man and His Work* (Washington, D.C.: U.S. Government Printing Office, 1968), pp. 156–57.

16. "The Vocational Education Act of 1963," *School Life* 46, no. 5 (March–April 1964): 3; James A. Parker, "Modern Trends in Industrial Arts and Vocational Education," *Industrial Arts and Vocational Education* 43, no. 6 (June 1954): 199.

17. John A. Beaumont, "Preparatory Education for Careers in Distribution," *Business Education Forum* 18, no. 7 (April 1964): 7; Ralph E. Mason, "Vocational Education for the Business Market," *High School Journal* 52, no. 5 (February 1969): 230.

18. U.S. Department of Health, Education, and Welfare, *Education for a Changing World of Work*, pp. 25–26; Layton S. Hawkins, Charles A. Prosser, and John C. Wright, *Development of Federal Legislation for Vocational Education*, comp. by J. Chester Swanson (Chicago: American Technical Society, 1966), p. 112; *Area Redevelopment Act, Statutes at Large* 75, sec. 16(a), 58–59, sec. 17 (a–e), 59–60 (1961).

19. Hawkins et al., *Development of Federal Legislation for Vocational Education*, pp. 112–13; *Federal Role in Education*, pp. 11–12; *Manpower Development and Training Act of 1962, Statutes at Large* 76, Title II, sec. 201–4, 25–29 (1965).

20. U.S. Department of Health, Education, and Welfare, *Education for a Changing World of Work*, pp. 27.

21. Venn, *Man, Education, and Work*, pp. 120–21.

22. Ibid., pp. 121–22.

23. U.S. Department of Health, Education, and Welfare, *Education for a Changing World of Work*, p. v; Elaine Exton, "Study of the President's Panel on Vocational Education," *Industrial Arts and Vocational Education* 52, no. 2 (February 1963): 52 p. 12.

24. U. S., Department of Health, Education, and Welfare, *Education for a Changing World of Work*, p. xvii.

25. Ibid., pp. xviii–xx, 224–45, 225–65.

26. *Federal Role in Education*, p. 11; Hollis Guy, "A Report to Members of NBEA," *Business Education Forum* 18, no. 3 (December 1963): 1–2; Paul S. Lomax, Russell J. Hosler, and Hamden L. Forkner, "The Vocational Act of 1963 and Suggested Lines of Action Relating to Vocational Education for Business and Office Occupations," *Business Education Forum* 18, no. 4 (January 1964): 29.

27. Elaine Exton, "The New Vocational Education Law," *Industrial Arts and Vocational Education* 53, no. 4 (April 1964): 22–23; *Vocational Education Act 1963*, *Statutes at Large* 77, sec. 4, 405 (1963).

28. Exton, "The New Vocational Education Law," p. 23; *Vocational Education Act of 1963*, *Statutes at Large* 77, (1963).

29. Theodor Schuchat, "The Vocational Education Act of 1963: What's in It for You?" *School Shop* 23, no. 8 (April 1964): 30; Venn, *Man, Education, and Work*, pp. 124–25; *Vocational Education Act of 1963*, *Statutes at Large* 77, sec. 10, 410–11 (1963).

30. Carl L. Byerly, "VEA '63 Holds Unusual Implications for Large Cities," *School Shop* 23, no. 8 (April 1964): 40; Schuchat, "The Vocational Education Act of 1963: What's in It for You?", p. 30.

31. *Vocational Education Act of 1963*, *Statutes at Large* 77, sec. 12, 411–12 (1963).

32. Walter M. Arnold and Edwin L. Rumpt, "A Master Catalyst—The Vocational Education Act of 1963," *School Shop* 25, no. 8 (April 1966): 49–50; U.S. Department of Health, Education, and Welfare, *Vocational Education*, pp. xxx–xxxii; U.S. Department of Health, Education, and Welfare, *Digest of Education Statistics*, *1975 Edition*, by W. Vance Grant and C. George Lind (Washington, D.C.: U.S. Government Printing Office, 1976), p. 138.

33. U.S. Department of Health, Education, and Welfare, *Vocational Education*, p. 16.

34. Harland E. Samson and David A. Thompson, "High School Preparatory Education for Careers in Distribution," *Business Education Forum* 18, no. 7 (April 1964): 10; James L. Blue, "The Spur that D. E. Needed: The Vocational Education Act of 1963," *Business Education World* 46, no. 1 (September 1965): 22–23.

35. U.S. Department of Health, Education, and Welfare, *Vocational Education*, p. 32.

36. *Federal Role in Education*, pp. 12–13.

37. Ibid., p. 13; U.S. Department of Health, Education, and Welfare, *Vocational Education*, p. 174.

38. *Federal Role in Education*, p. 13; U.S. Department of Health, Education, and Welfare, *Vocational Education*, p. 177.

39. U.S. Department of Health, Education, and Welfare, *Vocational Education*, pp. 175–177.

40. Ibid., pp. iii–iv; Lawrence W. Prakken, "Another Milestone in Vocational Education?" *School Shop* 27, no. 6 (February 1968): 2.

41. U.S. Department of Health, Education, and Welfare, *Vocational Education*, pp. xxvii, xxix; Prakken, "Another Milestone in Vocational Education?", p. 2; Theodor Schuchat, "Urges Budget Hike to $1.5 Billion; Recommends New 'All-in-One' Law," *School Shop* 27, no. 6 (February 1958): 39.

42. U. S., Department of Health, Education, and Welfare, *Vocational Education*, pp. xxvii–xxx.

43. Walter M. Arnold, "Washington Report," *Industrial Arts and Vocational Education* 57, no. 7 (September 1968): 1; Glenn I. Newhouse, "National Scene," *Industrial Arts and Vocational Education* 58, no. 2 (February 1969): p. 3; "Vocational Education," *Congressional Quarterly* 26, no. 30, July 26, 1968, pp. 1941–43; "Public Laws," *Congressional Quarterly* no. 45, November 8, 1968, p. 3108.

44. *Vocational Education Amendments of 1968*, Statutes at Large 82, sec. 102(a), 1064 (1968); Roberts, *Vocational and Practical Arts Education*, p. 120.

45. *Department of Labor, and Health, Education, and Welfare Appropriations Act, 1960, Statutes at Large* 82, Title II (1968); *Office of Education and Related Agencies Appropriations Act, 1972, Statutes at Large* 85, Title I (1971).

46. *Vocational Education Amendments of 1968*, Statutes at Large 82 (1968).

47. Theodor Schuchat, "From Washington," *School Shop* 28, no. 4 (December 1968): 74, 76: *Vocational Education Amendments of 1968*, Statutes at Large 82, (1968).

48. *Vocational Education Amendments of 1968*, Statutes at Large 82 (1968).

49. Melvin L. Barlow, "200 Years of Vocational Education, 1776–1976," *American Vocational Journal* 51, no. 5 (May 1976): 85.

50. Walter M. Arnold, "Landmark Education Bill Extends Vocational Funding," *Industrial Education* 61, no. 6 (September 1972): 7, 63; *Educational Amendments of 1972, Statutes at Large* 86, Title II, 325–26 (1972).

51. *Educational Amendments of 1976, Statutes at Large*, 90, Title II, sec. 201–4, 2168–2215 (1976); "Provisions of the New Voc Ed Amendments," *American Vocational Journal* 51, no. 8 (November 1976): 33–34; Lowell A. Burkett, "Latest Word from Washington," *American Vocational Journal* 51, no. 9 (December 1976): 9.

52. U.S. Department of Health, Education, and Welfare, Office of Education, *Work in America, Report of a Special Task Force to the Secretary of Health, Education, and Welfare, 1972* (Washington, D.C.: U.S. Government Printing Office, 1972 (reprinted by MIT Press, 1973), pp. 10–23, 134–52.

53. Ibid., 134.

54. Ibid., pp. 138–40.

55. Po-yen Koo, "Work in America: Attack and Rebuttal," *American Vocational Journal* 48, no. 5 (May 1973): 79–82.

56. Kenneth J. Rabben, "GAO Report on Voc Ed Stirs Controversy," *American Vocational Journal* 50, no. 3 (March 1975): 36–37; Carl F. Lamar, "GAO Review Misses the Mark", *American Vocational Journal* 50, no. 4 (April 1975): 42; U.S. Congress, General Accounting Office, *What is the Role of Federal Assistance for Vocational Education?* A Report by the General Accounting Office, 1975, reprinted in U.S. Congress, House, Committee on Education, *H. R. 19 and Related Bills to Amend the Vocational Act of 1963, Hearings before the Subcommittee on Elementary, Secondary, and Vocational Education,* House of Representatives, 94th Cong., 1st. sess., 1975, p. 10.

57. Rabben, "GAO Report on Voc Ed Stirs Controversy," p. 38; Lamar, "GAO Review Misses the Mark," pp. 42–44; John F. Jennings, "Emerging Issues in Vocational Education," *American Vocational Journal* 50, no. 6 (September 1975): 30; U.S. Congress, General Accounting Office, *What is the Role of Federal Assistance for Vocational Education?* pp. 14, 19–20, 46.

58. Rabben, "GAO Report on Voc Ed Stirs Controversy," p. 39.

59. Lamar, "GAO Review Misses the Mark," pp. 43–44.

60. Barlow, "200 Years of Vocational Education, 1776–1976," p. 86; Hugh Calkins, "The First Annual Report of the National Advisory Council on Vocational Education," *School Shop* 29, no. 3 (November 1969): 10, 12.

61. "Marland on Career Education," *American Education* 7, no. 9 (November 1971): 25–26; Lowell A. Burkett, "Latest Word from Washington," *American Vocational Jour-*

nal 46, no. 7 (October 1971): 10; Barlow, "200 Years of Vocational Education, 1776–1976," pp. 86.

62. Barlow, "200 Years of Vocational Education, 1776–1976," p. 86; *Education Amendments of 1974, Statutes at Large* 88, sec. 406, 551–53 (1974); *Educational Amendments of 1976, Statutes at Large* 90, Title III, sec. 331–36, 2221–24 (1976).

63. *Education Amendments of 1974, Statutes at Large* 88, sec. 406, 551–53 (1974).

64. Barlow, "200 Years of Vocational Education, 1776–1976," pp. 86–87; *Career Education Incentive Act, Statutes at Large* 91, 1464–74 (1977).

65. U.S. Department of Health, Education, and Welfare, Office of Education, National Advisory Council on Vocational Education, *Overview, 1975 Reports, State Advisory Councils on Vocational Education* (Washington, D.C.: National Advisory Council on Vocational Education, 1976), p. 5.

66. U.S. Department of Health, Education, and Welfare, *Work in America*, pp. 140–144.

67. Grant Venn, "Career Education: Not a Panacea," *Business Education Forum* 27, no. 2 (November 1972): 3–4; M. L. Story, "Vocational Education as Contemporary Slavery," *The Education Digest* 40, no. 1 (September 1974): 6–9; Jerome A. Wray, "Vocational Education—Of What Value?" *National Association of Secondary School Principals, Bulletin* 60, no. 404 (December 1976): 60–62; William B. Seccurro, "Vocational Education—Meeting Today's Demands," *National Association of Secondary-School Principals, Bulletin* 61, no. 406 (February 1977): pp. 100–102.

68. Grant, *Digest of Education Statistics, 1975 Edition*, p. 139; U.S. Department of Health, Education, and Welfare, Office of Education, *Annual Evaluation Report on Programs Administered by the U.S. Office of Education FY 1975*, (Washington, D.C.: Office of Planning, Budgeting, and Evaluation, 1975), p. 225, (ERIC ED 125 109).

69. Tonne, "Three Cheers for McCargo!" pp. 286–87; Warren Meyer and Lorraine T. Furtado, "A Historical Development of Distributive Education," appears as Chapter 3 of the *National Business Education Yearbook, Number 14* (Reston, Va.: National Business Education Association, 1976), pp. 54–55; Carl T. Brown, "Distributive Education on the Upswing: A History," *American Vocational Journal* 51, no. 9 (December 1976): 36.

70. "Distributive Educators Share Ideas—and Ideals," *American Vocational Journal* 52, no. 2 (February 1977): 48–49.

71. Grant, *Digest of Education Statistics, 1975 Edition*, p. 138; *The DECA Handbook*, p. 16.

72. Grant, *Digest of Education Statistics, 1975 Edition*, p. 139.

73. U.S. Department of Health, Education, and Welfare, *Vocational Education*, p. 40; U.S. Department of Health, Education, and Welfare, Office of Education, *Vocational and Technical Education, Annual Report, Fiscal Year 1969* (Washington, D.C.: Government Printing Office, 1971), p. 75.

74. U.S. Department of Health, Education, and Welfare, *Work in America*, p. 149.

75. Douglas Adamson, "Pressure for Change in Distributive Education," *Business Education Forum* 28, no. 5 (February 1974): 45; Jack L. Meiss, "Career Education: Implications for Distributive Education," *Business Education Forum* 29, no. 1 (October 1974): 23–25.

76. Wilma Jean Alexander, et al. *Business Education into the Eighties* (Springfield: Illinois State University, 1979), p. 220.

77. Mary A. Golladay and Rolf M. Wulfsberg. *The Condition of Vocational Education* (Washington, D.C.: U.S. Government Printing Office, 1981), p. 13.

78. Ibid., pp. 25, 37.

79. Ibid., pp. 129, 134.

80. National Commission for Employment Policy, *The Federal Role in Vocational*

Education (Washington, D.C.: National Commission for Employment Policy, 1981), pp. 2–3, 8–9; *Omnibus Budget Reconciliation Act, 1981, Public Law 97–35* (1981).

81. Gene Bottoms, "What the New Federalism Means to Voc Ed." *Voc Ed*, *Journal of the American Vocational Association* 57, no. 3, (April 1982): pp. 10–11.

82. Tony Rodasta. "Reganonmics—What Effect Is It Having on Vocational Education and Marketing and Distributive Education?" *Marketing Educator's News* I, no. 1, (Fall 1981): 11; John Feirer, "Voc Ed and the New Administration," *Industrial Education* 70, no. 8 (November 1981): 4–6.

83. Grant, *Digest of Education Statistics, 1975 ed.*, p. 139; Golladay and Wulfsberg, *The Condition of Vocational Education*, pp. 25, 37, 129.

84. Ibid.

Bibliography

Act to Promote the Fishing Industry in the United States and its Territories by Providing for the Training of Needed Personnel for Such Industry. Statutes at Large, vol. 70 (1956).

Act to Provide for Further Development of Vocational Education in the Several States and Territories (George-Deen Act). *Statutes at Large*, vol. 45 (1929).

Act to Provide for Further Development of Vocational Education in the Several States and Territories (George-Ellzey Act). *Statutes at Large*, vol. 48 (1934).

Act to Provide for the Further Development of Vocational Education in the Several States and Territories (George-Deen Act). *Statutes at Large*, vol. 49 (1936).

Act to Provide for the Promotion of Vocational Rehabilitation of Persons Disabled in Industry (Smith-Fess Act). *Statues at Large*, vol. 41 (1920).

Adamson, Douglas. "Pressures for Change in Distributive Education." *Business Education Forum*, 28, no. 5 (February 1974): 44–45.

"The Administration of the Smith-Hughes Act." *School and Society* 6, no. 151, November 17, 1917, pp. 594–96.

Agriculture Experiment Stations (Adams Act). *U.S. Code*, Vol. 1 (1958).

Alexander, Wilma Jean, *et al. Business Education into the Eighties*. Springfield: Illinois State University, 1979.

Amendment to the Agricultural Colleges Act of 1890 (Nelson Amendment). *U.S. Code*, vol. 1 (1970).

American Education in the Postwar Period. Part I, *Curriculum Reconstruction*. Edited by Nelson B. Henry. Forty-fourth Yearbook, National Society for the Study of Education. Chicago: University of Chicago Press, 1945.

Area Redevelopment Act. Statutes at Large, vol. 85 (1961).

Arnold, Walter M. "Washington Report." *Industrial Arts and Vocational Education* 57, no. 7 (September 1968): 1, 4.

———. "Landmark Education Bill Extends Vocational Funding," *Industrial Education* 61, no. 6 (September 1972): 63–64.

———, and Rumpf, Edwin L. "A Master Catalyst—The Vocational Education Act of 1963." *School Shop* 25, no. 8 (April 1966): 49–51.

Arthur, Charles M. "Vocational Education." *Congressional Digest* 13, no. 8–9, (August-September 1934): 199–200.

———. "George-Deen Act and Its Implications." *School Life* 22, no. 5 (January 1937): 133–34.

"A. V. A. Defends Earmarked Funds." *Nation's Schools* 43, no. 1 (January 1949): 50.

151

Axt, Richard G. *The Federal Government and Financing Higher Education.* New York: Columbia University Press, 1952.

"The Barden Vocational Education Bill." *Journal of Business Education* 21, no. 4 (December 1945): 26–27.

Barlow, Melvin L. *History of Industrial Education in the United States.* Peoria, Ill.: Charles A. Bennett Company, 1967.

———. "200 Years of Vocational Education, 1776–1976." *American Vocational Journal* 51, no. 5 (May 1976): 21–88.

Bauder, Charles Franklin. "Vocational Education and the New Deal." *Industrial Education Magazine* 37, no. 3 (May 1935): 135–36.

Bawden, William T. "The Federal Board for Vocational Education." *Manual Training Magazine* 19, no. 1 (September 1917): 1–4.

———. "Some Leaders in Industrial Education (Part I)." *Industrial Arts and Vocational Education* 40, no. 2 (February 1951): 52–55.

———. "Some Leaders in Industrial Education (Part II)." 40, no. 4 (April 1951): 147–50.

Beaumont, John A. "The Federal Role in Distributive Education." *American Vocational Journal* 38, no. 9 (December 1963): 36–37.

———. "Preparatory Education for Careers in Distribution." *Business Education Forum* 18, no. 7 (April 1964): 7–9.

Beckley, Donald K. "Early Days in Retail Training." *Business Education World* 29, no. 1 (September 1948): 38–41.

Bennett, Charles Alpheus. *History of Manual and Industrial Education up to 1870.* Peoria, Ill.: The Manual Arts Press, 1926.

———. *History of Manual and Industrial Education, 1870 to 1917.* Peoria, Ill.: Charles A. Bennett Company, 1937.

"Bill to Provide Additional Federal Aid for Vocational Education." *Higher Education* 1, no. 10, May 15, 1945, pp. 6–7.

Blue, James L. "The Spur that D. E. Needed: The Vocational Education Act of 1963." *Business Education World* 46, no. 1 (September 1965): 22–23, 35.

Bottoms, Gene. "What the New Federalism Means to Voc Ed." *Voc Ed. Journal of the American Vocational Association* 57, no. 3 (April 1982): 10–11.

"A Brief History of the U.S. Office of Education." *Business Education World* 26, no. 7 (March 1946): 396.

Brown, T. Carl. "Distributive Education on the Upswing: A History." *American Vocational Journal* 51, no. 9 (December 1976): 36–38, 42.

———, and Logan, William B., eds. "Fifty Years of Progress in Distributive Education." *American Vocational Journal* 31, no. 9 (December 1956): 57–59, 62–66, 111.

Burkett, Lowell A. "Latest Word from Washington." *American Vocational Journal* 46, no. 7 (October 1971): 9–10.

———. "Latest Word from Washington." *American Vocational Journal* 51, no. 9, (December 1976), 9–10.

Byerly, Carl L. "VEA '63 Holds Unusual Implications for Large Cities." *School Shop* 23, no. 8, (April 1964): 40–41.

Calkins, Hugh. "The First Annual Report of the National Advisory Council on Vocational Education." *School Shop* 29, no. 3, (November 1969), 2, 10, 12.

Career Education Incentive Act, Statutes at Large 91, (1977).

Clift, Virgil A.; Anderson, Archibald W.; and Hullfist, H. Gordon, eds. *Negro Education in America: Its Adequacy, Problems, and Needs.* Sixteenth Yearbook of the John Dewey Society. New York: Harper, 1962.

"Commercial Education." *Cyclopedia of Education.* 1911, vol. 2.

Cooper, W. John, "Office of Education." *Scientific Monthly* 26, no. 2, (February 1933): 121–30.

Cremin, Lawrence A. *The Transformation of the School: Progressivism in American Education, 1876–1957.* New York: Alfred A. Knopf, 1961.

"A Criticism of the George-Deen Vocational Education Act." *Elementary School Journal* 37, no. 7 (March 1937): 488–90.

Cross, Jeanie. "Simulated Stores Stimulate Learning: Many Examples Presented at Anaheim." *American Vocational Journal* 51, no. 2 (February 1976): 45–47.

Curoe, Phillip R. V. *Educational Attitudes and Policies of Organized Labor in the United States.* New York: Teachers College, Columbia University, 1926.

Curti, Merle. *Social Ideas of American Educators: Report of the American Historical Association Commission on the Social Studies,* Part 10. New York: Charles Scribner's Sons, 1935.

David, Henry. "The NIE Report on Vocational Education." *Voc Ed, Journal of the American Vocational Association,* 57, no. 1 (January–February 1982): 48–51.

D. E. Future Exploding in Congress." *Business Education World* 31, no. 10 (June 1951): 489.

Dennis, L. H. "The New George-Barden Vocational Education Act." *Industrial Arts and Vocational Education* 35, no. 9 (November 1946): 18A.

Departments of Labor, and Health, Education, and Welfare Appropriations Act, 1969. Statutes at Large, vol. 82 (1968).

Departments of Labor, and Health, Education and Welfare, and Related Agencies Appropriations Act, 1954. Statutes at Large 67 (1953).

Departments of Labor, and Health, Education, and Welfare, and Related Agencies Appropriations Act, 1955. Statutes at Large, 68 (1954).

Departments of Labor, and Health, Education, and Welfare, and Related Agencies Appropriations Act, 1956. Statutes At Large 69 (1955).

Distributive Education Clubs of America, Inc. *The DECA Handbook, 1975 Revised.* Washington, D.C.: The Distributive Education Clubs of America, Inc., 1975.

"Distributive Educators Share Ideas—and Ideals." *American Vocational Journal,* no. 2 (February 1977): 48–51.

Dugger, Roy. "The Vocational Act of 1963." *National Association of Secondary School Principals, Bulletin* 49, 301 (May 1965): 5–23.

Education Amendments of 1974. Statutes at Large 88 (1974).

Education Amendments of 1972. Statutes at Large 86 (1972).

Education Amendments of 1976. Statutes at Large 90 (1976).

Employment Act of 1946. Statutes at Large, vol. 40 (1946).

Exton, Elaine. "The Federal Security Agency Attains Cabinet Rank." *School Board Journal* (May 1953): 45–46, 98, 100.

———. "A Progress Report on Vocational Education." *Industrial Arts and Vocational Education*, 49, no. 1 (January 1960): 18–19, 51.

———. "The New Vocational Education Law." *Industrial Arts and Vocational Education* 53, no. 4 (April 1964): 22–24.

———. "Study of the President's Panel on Vocational Education." *Industrial Arts and Vocational Education* 52, no. 2 (February 1973): 12.

"The Federal Plan for Vocational Education." *Survey* 35, no. 24, March 11, 1916, 692.

Federal Role in Education. Washington, D.C.: Congressional Quarterly Service, 1965.

"The Federal Subsidy to Vocational Education." *Industrial Arts Magazine*, 15, no. 3 (March 1926): 101–2.

Feirer, John. "Voc Ed and the New Administration." *Industrial Education* 70, no. 8 (November 1981): 4, 6.

First Supplemental Civil Functions Appropriations Act, 1941. Statutes at Large, vol. 54 (1940).

"The Forward March in Vocational Education." *School Life* 21, no. 6 (Feburary 1936): 152–53, 168.

George, Walter Franklin. *Current Biography, 1943*. New York: H. H. Wilson, 1944.

———. *Biographical Dictionary of the American Congress, 1774–1949*. Washington, D.C.: Government Printing Office, 1950.

Golladay, Mary A., and Wulfsberg, Rolf M. *The Condition of Vocational Education*. Washington, D.C.: Government Printing Office, 1981.

Good, H. G. *A History of American Education*. 2d. ed. New York: Macmillan, 1962.

Gordon, I. Swanson, ed. *The Future of Vocational Education*. Arlington, Va.: American Vocational Association, 1981.

Grace, Alonzo G. "Vocational Education and the Post-War Period." *Education* 66, no. 4 (December 1945): 228–32.

Guy, Hollis. "A Report to Members of NBEA." *Business Education Forum* 18, no. 3 (December 1963): 1–2.

Hatch Act. U.S. Code, vol. 1 (1970).

Hawkins, Layton S.; Prosser, Charles A.; and Wright, John C. *Development of Vocational Education*. Chicago: American Technical Society, 1951.

———. *Development of Federal Legislation for Vocational Education*. Comp. by J. Chester Swanson. Chicago: American Technical Society, 1966.

Health Amendments Act of 1956. Statutes at Large, 70 (1956).

Hughes, Dudley Mayes. *Biographical Dictionary of the American Congress. 1774–1927*. Washington, D.C.: U.S. Government Printing Office, 1928.

"Increased Federal Aid of D. E. Seems Likely." *Journal of Business Education.* 28, no. 8 (May 1953): 348.

Ivins, Wilson H., and Runge, William B. *Work Experience in High School.* New York: Ronald Press, 1951.

Jennings, John F. "Emerging Issues in Vocational Education." *American Vocational Journal* 50, no. 6 (September 1975): 29–32.

Kandel, Isaac Leon. *Federal Aid for Vocational Education, A Report to the Carnegie Foundation for the Advancement of Teaching.* Bulletin no. 10. New York: Carnegie Foundation for the Advancement of Teaching, 1917.

—————.*The Impact of the War Upon American Education.* Chapel Hill: University of North Carolina Press, 1948.

Koo, Po-yen. "Work in America: Attack and Rebuttal." *American Vocational Journal* 48, no. 5 (May 1973): 79–82, 101.

Kyker, B. Frank. "Five Years of Distributive Education Under the George-Deen Art." *National Business Education Quarterly* 11, no. 3 (March 1943): 13–16, 59.

Lamar, Carl F. "GAO Review Misses the Mark." *American Vocational Journal* 50, no. 4 (April 1975): 42–45.

Land Grant Colleges Act (First Morrill Act). *U.S. Code*, vol. 1 (1970).

Lehman, Clarence D. "How the Smith-Hughes Act Affects Vocational Expenditure." *Nation's Schools* 7, no. 5 (May 1931): 41–43.

Lomax, Paul S.; Hosler, Russell J.; and Forkner, Hamden L. "The Vocational Act of 1963 and Suggested Lines of Action Relating to Vocational Education for Business and Office Occupations." *Business Education Forum* 18, no. 4 (January 1964): 29–32.

Lu. Hsien. *Federal Role in Education: A Comprehensive Study of Federal Relations to Education in the United States—Their Past, Present, and Future.* New York: American Press, 1968.

McClure, Arthur F. *The Truman Administration and the Problems of Post-War Labor, 1945–1948.* Rutherford, N. J.: Fairleigh Dickinson University Press, 1968.

Manpower Development and Training Act of 1962. Statutes at Large 76, (1965).

"Marland on Career Education." *American Education* 7, no. 9 (November 1971): 25–28.

Mason, Ralph E. "Vocational Education for the Business Market." *High School Journal* 52, no. 5 (February 1969): 229–224.

Meiss, Jack L. "Career Education: Implications for Distributive Eduation." *Business Education Forum* 29, no. 1 (October 1974): 23–25.

Meyer, Warren, and Furtado, Lorraine T. "A Historical Development of Distributive Education." *Fourteenth Yearbook of the National Business Education Association.* Reston, Va.: National Business Education Association, 1976.

Mobley, M. D. "Vocational Education and Full Employment." *Education* 66, no. 4 (December 1945): 197–204.

Moehlman, Arthur B. "Vocational Bills Threaten Balance and Unity of Secondary Education." *Nation's Schools* 34, no. 5 (November 1944): 19.

National Commission for Employment Policy. *The Federal Role in Vocational Education.* Washington, D.C.: National Commission for Employment Policy, 1981.

National Defense Education Act of 1958. Statutes at Large 72 (1958).

Newham, Irl S. "The Historical Development of the Distributive Education Clubs of America." Master's thesis, Central Missouri State University, 1966.

Newhouse, Glenn I. "National Scene." *Industrial Arts and Vocational Education* 58, no. 2 (February 1969): 3–4.

Nichols, Frederick G. "Vocational Training for the Distributive Occupations Under the George-Deen Act." *Education Digest* 3, no. 5 (January 1938): 4–7.

———. "The Background of Distributive Education." *National Business Education Quarterly* 2, no. 2 (March 1943): 9–12, 44–46, 48, 50.

———. "Business Education—Clerical and Distributive." *National Society for Study of Education.* Forty-second Yearbook, Part I, Chicago: University of Chicago Press, 1943.

Nystrom, Dennis C., and Bayne, G. Keith. *Occupation and Career Education Legislation, 2d ed.* Indianapolis: Bobbs-Merrill Educational Publishing, 1979.

Office of Education and Related Agencies appropriations Act, 1972. Statutes at Large 85 (1971).

Omnibus Budget Reconciliation Act, 1981, Public Law 97–35 (1981).

Parker, James A. "Modern Trends in Industrial Arts and Vocational Education." *Industrial Arts and Vocational Education* 43, no. 6 (June 1954): 199–201.

Patch, Buel W. "Full Employment." *Editorial Research Reports* 2, no. 4 July 30, 1945, pp. 61–78.

Prakken, Lawrence W. "Another Milestone in Vocational Education?" *School Shop* 27, no. 6 (February 1968): 2.

———. "The Future of Federal Funding." *School Shop* 41, no. 4 (November 1981), p. 2.

"President Roosevelt's Message on the Congressional Appropriation for Vocational Education." *School and Society* 46, no. 1182 (August 21, 1937), pp. 249–51.

Prince, Lucinda W. "Training for Efficiency in the Department Store." *Bookman* 43 (April 1916): 190–93.

"Progress of Vocational Education Programs: States Overmatch Federal Grants." *Education for Victory* 1, no. 32, June 15, 1943, pp. 23–26.

"Provisions of the New Voc Ed Amendments." *American Vocational Journal* 51, no. 8 (November 1976), 33–34.

"Public Law." *Congressional Quarterly* 26, no. 45. November 8, 1968, pp. 3106–3109.

Rabben, Kenneth J. "GAO Report on Voc Ed Stirs Controversy." *American Vocational Journal* 50, no. 3 (March 1975): 36–39, 62–63.

Roberts, Roy W. *Vocational and Practical Arts Education: History, Development, and Principles.* 3rd Ed. New York: Harper & Row, 1971.

Rodasta, Tony. "Reaganomics—What Effect Is It Having on Vocational Education and Marketing and Distributive Education?" *Marketing Educator's News* 1, no. 1 (Fall 1981): 11.

Roley, Dennis E. "The Prospects Are Bright." *Business Education Forum* 22, no. 8 (May 1968): 7–8.

Samson, Harland E. et, al. *National Conference on Marketing and Distributive Education: Directions for the 1970's*. Reston, Va.: Marketing and Distributive Education Association, 1980.

————, and Thompson, David A. "High School Preparatory Education for Careers in Distribution." *Business Education Forum* 18, no. 7 (April 1964): 10–12.

Sawyer, Ruth. "Have You Met Mrs. Prince?" *Good Housekeeping* 72, (January 1921): 57, 118–21.

Schuchat, Theodor. "The Vocational Education Act of 1963: What's in It for You?" *School Shop* 23, no. 8 (April 1964): 30–34, 125.

————. "Urges Budget Hike to $1.5 Billion; Recommends New 'All-in-One' Law." *School Shop* 27, no. 6 (February 1968): 39–40.

————. "From Washington." *School Shop* 28, no. 4 (December 1968): 80, 72, 73–74, 76.

Scott, Cecil Winfield and Hill, Clyde M. eds. *Public Education Under Criticism*. New York: Prentice-Hall, 1954.

Seccurro, William B. "Vocational Education—Meeting Today's Demands." *National Association of Secondary-School Principals*, Bulletin 61, no. 406 (February 1977): 100–102.

Second Deficiency Appropriations Act, 1940. Statutes at Large, vol. 54 (1940).

"Sixth Report of the National Advisory Council on Vocational Education— Counseling and Guidance: A Call for Change." *Business Education Forum* 27, no. 2 (November 1972): 4–6.

Smith, Hoke. *Biographical Dictionary of the American Congress, 1774–1949*. Washington, D.C.: U.S. Government Printing Office, 1950.

"The Smith-Hughes Act." *Industrial Arts Magazine* 6, no. 4 (April 1917): 168–69.

Snedden, David. "Vocational Education: Next Stages." *School and Society*, 46, no. 1200. December 25, 1937, pp. 813–18.

————. "Vocational Education: Another Milestone?" *School and Society* 49, no. 1275, June 3 1393, pp. 685–691.

"Statement of Dr. Paul H. Nystrom at the Hearings for the Vocational Education Bill." *Journal of Business Education* 21, no. 3 (November 1945): 26–27.

Stockwell, Lynn E. "Federal Aid to Vocational Education." *Industrial Education Magazine* 38, no. 6 (December 1926): 179–80.

Story, M. L. "Vocational Education as Contemporary Slavery." *The Education Digest* 40, no. 1 (September 1974): 6–9.

"Testimony on the Vocational Education Bill." *Journal of Business Education* 21, no. 2 (October 1945): 28–29.

"Testimony on the Vocational Education Bill." *Journal of Business Education* 21, no. 6 (January 1946): 29.

Tonne, Herbert A. "Senate Vocational Education Bill Hearings." *Journal of Business Education* 21, no. 1 (September 1945): 34.

———. "Three Cheers for McCargo!" *Journal of Business Education* 38, no. 7 (April 1953): 286–287.

U.S. Congress. General Accounting Office. *What Is the Role of Federal Assistance for Vocational Education?* A Report by the General Accounting Office, 1975. Reprinted in U.S. Congress. House. Committee on Education. *H.R. 19 And Related Bills to Amend the Vocational Act of 1963, Hearings*, before the Subcommittee on Elementary, Secondary, and Vocational Education, House of Representatives, 94th Cong., 1st sess., 1975.

U.S. Congress. House. Debate on H.R. 12120. 74th Cong., 2nd sess., May 26, 1936. *Congressional Record* 80, 7954–78.

U.S. Congress. House. Debate on Amendments to Department of the Interior Appropriations Bill, 1938. 74th Cong., 1st sess., May 20, 1937. *Congressional Record* 81, 4849–63.

U.S. Congress. Senate. Letter from L. J. Taber, Master, National Grange Supporting S. 2883. 74th Cong., 2nd sess., Februrary 18, 1936. *Congressional Record* 80, 2279.

U.S. Congress. Senate. Joint Resolution of the Legislature of the State of Wisconsin Urging the Congress of the United States to Allocate to the States the Whole Appropriations Authorized by the George-Deen Act for Vocational Education. 75th Cong., 1st sess., February 23, 1937. *Congressional Record* 81, 1467.

U.S. Congress. Senate. Debate on H.R. 6958, Department of the Interior Appropriations. 75th Cong., 1st sess., June 28, 1937. *Congressional Record* 81, 6389–6406.

U.S. Department of Health, Education, and Welfare. Office of Education. *Education for a Changing World of Work: Report of the Panel of Consultants on Vocational Education.* Washington, D.C.: U.S. Government Printing Office, 1963.

———. National Advisory Council on Vocational Education. *Vocational Education: The Bridge Between Man and His Work.* Washington, D.C.: U.S. Government Printing Office, 1968.

———. *Vocational and Technical Education, Annual Report, Fiscal Year 1969.* Washington D.C.: U.S. Government Printing Office, 1971.

———. *Work in America, Report of a Special Task Force to the Secretary of Health, Education, and Welfare, 1972.* Washington, D.C.: U.S. Government Printing Office, 1972. (Cambridge, Massas.: Press, 1973).

———. *Annual Evaluation Report on Programs Administered by the U.S. Office of Education FY 1975.* Washington, D.C.: Office of Planning, Budgeting and Evaluation, 1975.

———. *Digest of Education Statistics, 1975 Edition*, by W. Vance Grant and C. George Lind. Washington, D.C.: U.S. Government Printing Office, 1976.

———. National Advisory Council on Vocational Education. *Overview, 1975 Reports, State Advisory Councils on Vocational Education.* Washington, D.C.: National Advisory Council on Vocational Education, 1976.

U.S. Department of the Interior. Office of Education. *Federal Cooperation in*

Agricultural Extension Work, Vocational Education, and Vocational Rehabilitation, by Lloyd E. Blauch. Bulletin no. 15. Washington, D.C.: U.S. Government Printing Office, 1933 (reprinted by Arno Press and New York Times in 1969).

———. *Cooperative Training in Retail Selling in the Public Schools,* by Glenn Oscar Emick. Vocational Division Bulletin 186, Commercial No. Series 10. Washington, D.C.: U.S. Government Printing Office, 1936 (1937).

———. *Statement of Policies for the Administration of Vocational Education.* Vocational Education Bulletin No. 1 (Revised, February 1937). Washington, D.C.: U.S. Government Printing Office, 1937.

———. *Vocational, Education and Guidance of Negroes,* by Ambrose Caliver. Bulletin no. 38. Washington, D.C.: U.S. Government Printing Office, 1937.

———. *Vocational Education,* by John Dale Russell and associates. Staff Study No. 8. Washington, D.C.: U.S. Government Printing Office, 1938.

———. *Cooperative Part-Time Retail Training Programs: Supervision, Coordination, and Teaching, by Kenneth B. Hass. Vocational Division Bulletin 205, Business Education Series 12. Washington, D.C.: U.S. Government Printing Office, 1939.*

———. *Cooperative Part-Time Retail Training Programs: Supervision, Coordination, and Teaching,* by Kenneth B. Hass. Vocational Division Bulletin 205, Business Education Series 12. Washington, D.C.: U.S. Government Printing Office, 1939.

U.S. Department of the Interior. Office of Education. Advisory Committee on Education. *Special Programs of Negro Education,* by Doxey Alphonso Willkerson. Staff Study No. 12. Washington, D.C.: U.S. Government Printing Office, 1939.

———. *Distributive Education, Organization and Administration,* by Kenneth B. Haas. Vocational Division Bulletin 211; Business Education Series 13. Washington, D.C.: U.S. Government Printing Office, 1940.

———. *Vocational Training Problems When the War Ends,* by John C. Wright. Vocational Division Leaflet No. 12. Washington, D.C.: U.S. Government Printing Office, 1943.

———. *Vocational Education in the Years Ahead: A Report of a Committee to Study Postwar Problems in Vocational Education.* Vocational Division Bulletin No. 234; General Series No. 7. Washington, D.C.: U.S. Government Printing Office, 1945.

U.S. President. *Public Papers of the Presidents of the United States: Harry S. Truman, 1946.* Washington, D.C.: U.S. Government Printing Office, 1962.

Venn, Grant. *Man, Education, and Work: Postsecondary Vocational and Technical Education.* Washington, D.C.: American Council on Education, 1964.

———. "Career Education: Not a Panacea." *Business Education Forum* 27, no. 2 (November 1972): 3–4.

"Vocational Education." *Congressional Quarterly* 26, no. 30, July 16, 1968), pp. 1941–43.

Vocational Education Act of 1917 (Smith-Hughes Act). *Statutes at Large,* vol. 39 (1917).

Vocational Education Act of 1946. (George-Barden Act). *Statutes at Large,* vol.

60 (1946).

Vocational Education Act of 1963. Statutes at Large 77 (1963).

"The Vocational Education Act of 1963." *School Life* 46, no. 5, (March–April 1964): 3–12.

Vocational Education Amendments of 1968. Statutes at Large 82 (1968).

Vocational Rehabilitation Act (Smith-Sears Act). *Statutes at Large*, vol. 40 (1918).

Walker, Arthur L.; Huffman, Harry; and Beaumont, John A. eds. "Fifty Years of Progress in Business Education." *American Vocational Journal* 31, no. 9 (December 1956): 47–54.

Wanous, S. J. "A Chronology of Business Education in the United States." *Business Education Forum* 11, no. 8, the Centennial Issue (May 1957): 54–60.

"Wartime Distributive Education." Education for Victory 1, no. 11, August 1, 1942, p. 19.

Webb, Earl B. "Distributive Occupations Education Under the George-Deen Act." Chapter 19 of *Improvement of Classroom Teaching in Business Education*. Twelfth Yearbook of the Eastern. Commercial Teachers Association. Philadelphia: Eastern Commercial Teachers' Association, 1939.

Wendt, Erhard F. "Brief History of Industrial Arts and Vocational Education." Part I. *Industrial Arts and Vocational Education* 35, no. 4 (April 1946): 151–54.

———. "Brief History of Industrial Arts and Vocational Education." Part II. *Industrial Arts and Vocational Education* 35, no. 5 (May 1946): 202–3.

Williams, Rae C. "Thirty-Two Years in D.E." *Business Education World* 38, no. 5 (January 1953): 238.

Wirth, Arthur G. "Charles A. Prosser and the Smith-Hughes Act." *Educational Forum* 36, no. 3 (March 1972): 365–71.

Wray, Jerome A. "Vocational Education—Of What Value?" *National Association of Secondary-School Principals*, *Bulletin* 60, no. 404 (December 1976): 60–62.

Wright, John C. "Vocational Education and the National Welfare." *Education* 66, no. 4 (December 1945): 205–8.

Index